ESSENTIAL PSYCHOLOGY

General Editor
Peter Herriot

F2

THE PSYCHOLOGY OF HANDICAP

ESSENTIAL

PSYCHOLOGY

THE PSYCHOLOGY OF HANDICAP

Rosemary Shakespeare

Methuen

First published in 1975 by Methuen & Co. Ltd
11 New Fetter Lane, London EC4P 4EE
Reprinted 1982

Published in the USA by
Methuen & Co.
in association with Methuen, Inc.
733 Third Avenue, New York, NY 10017

© 1975 Rosemary Shakespeare
Printed in Great Britain by
Richard Clay (The Chaucer Press), Ltd
Bungay, Suffolk

ISBN (hardback) 0 416 81710 6
ISBN (paperback) 0 416 81720 3

We are grateful to Grant McIntyre of
Grant McIntyre Ltd for editorial assistance
in the preparation of this Series

Contents

Editor's introduction

Handicap is a subject we are slowly beginning to face up to. As a society, we probably congratulated ourselves when we started to think of handicapped people as ill rather than as victims of divine retribution. But it is slowly becoming clear that sympathy is not what handicapped people want and institutional provision is not necessarily what they need. Rather, we need to examine our own attitudes towards those who are different from ourselves; and we need to perceive clearly how we have projected these attitudes into the provision we make for the handicapped. Rosemary Shakespeare shows that careful research into a handicapped person's abilities is not enough. We must also discover his feelings about himself as an individual, his family, and our own reaction to him. This book provides a careful and thorough, and yet a compassionate account of what we know about the psychology of handicap.

The Psychology of Handicap belongs to Unit F of *Essential Psychology*. What unifies the books in this unit is the concept of change, not only in people but also in psychology. Both the theory and the practice of the subject are changing fast. The assumptions underlying the different theoretical frameworks are being revealed and questioned. New basic assumptions are being advocated, and consequently new frameworks constructed. One example is the theoretical framework of 'mental illness': the assumptions of normality and abnormality are being questioned, together with the notions of 'the cause', 'the cure', and 'the doctor–patient relationship'. As a result, different frameworks are developing, and different professional practices gradually being initiated. There are, though, various social and political structures which tend to inhibit the translation of changing theory into changing practice.

One interesting change is the current aversion to theoretical frameworks which liken human beings to something else. For example, among many psychologists the analogy of the human being as a computer which characterizes Unit A is in less favour than the concepts of development (Unit C) and the person (Unit D).

Essential Psychology as a whole is designed to reflect this changing structure and function of psychology. The authors are both academics and professionals, and their aim has been to introduce the most important concepts in their areas to beginning students. They have tried to do so clearly, but have not attempted to conceal the fact that concepts that now appear central to their work may soon be peripheral. In other words, they have presented psychology as a developing set of views of man, not as a body of received truth. Readers are not intended to study the whole series in order to 'master the basics'. Rather, since different people may wish to use different theoretical frameworks for their own purposes, the series has been designed so that each title stands on its own. But it is possible that if the reader has read no psychology before, he will enjoy individual books more if he has read the introductions (A1, B1 etc.) to the units to which they belong. Readers of the units concerned with applications of psychology (E, F) may benefit from reading all the introductions.

A word about references in the text to the work of other writers – e.g. 'Smith (1974)'. These occur where the author feels he must acknowledge an important concept or some crucial evidence by name. The book or article referred to will be listed in the References (which doubles as Name index) at the back of the book. The reader is invited to consult these sources if he wishes to explore topics further.

We hope you enjoy psychology.

Peter Herriot

1
The context
of handicap

Many conditions have been considered as handicapping; being a woman, being homosexual, being black, being a member of a minority religious group and many more minority characteristics have all been seen, in a wide sense, as handicapping. (See F8 in *Essential Psychology*.) In common with conditions seen as handicapping in a narrow sense, like blindness, deafness or physical and mental handicap, they can limit a person's opportunities, create prejudices in others and cause frustration.

In this volume we shall deal with handicap in the more restricted sense and limit discussion to three groups of conditions: handicaps with a primarily motor effect, such as cerebral palsy, limb deficiency and epilepsy; those with a mental, social or emotional effect such as mental handicap, mental illness or autism; and the sensory handicaps of deafness and blindness (see Appendix for brief description of terms used).

Fundamental to any study of handicap is the recognition that the handicapped person is a person first and foremost, and secondly has a handicap, which affects some, but rarely all aspects of his behaviour. A handicap is hardly ever total, except in the few cases where a physical and mental handicap combine and are of such severity that the person's behaviour is limited to an extent where it is totally different from any behaviour seen in the repertoire of a normal person. In every other case, the handicapped person has strengths and weaknesses, behaviours affected by the handicap and behaviours which are not. He may be unable to see but have no difficulty in moving around the house, he may be deaf but write poetry, he may be mentally handicapped but very good at football.

Handicaps cover a wide range of severity, from those so mild that only a small area of behaviour is affected to those which influence a large part of a person's life. 'The handicapped' spans a range of people from the person who is slightly deaf, has some weakness in a limb or is not quite intelligent enough to cope with the complications of everyday life, to the person who is mentally and physically so disabled that he needs assistance in all aspects of his life.

In general, we can regard all handicaps in terms of inadequate behavioural development or inadequate behavioural functioning in the way that a person interacts with his environment. That is, his handicap has either prevented him from making the normal responses to his surroundings or makes it impossible for him to do so even though he has at one time been capable. For example, our environment demands that we work and support ourselves financially. Because of his handicap, the disabled person has not been able to develop the necessary skills. Some handicapped people's skills will be far below the necessary developmental level, others will be close but not quite adequate. The person who becomes handicapped in later life, has at one time met the demands of the environment and worked to support himself, but his handicap now prevents him.

So to assess the degree of a person's handicap, we need to assess how many of the demands of his surroundings he fails to meet and how far removed from the normal level is his response.

No specific handicap implies specific problems. There are wide differences in the degree to which people learn to cope with the same degree of disability. For example one person, with a moderate degree of spasticity, may be living a normal life, working, pursuing hobbies and interests, making a wide range of friends, whilst another, with a similar handicap, may be living a restricted life at home with his parents.

People with handicaps are born fairly randomly into stable, loving families and into broken or rejecting ones. Some of a person's personality characteristics and problems will be due entirely to his background, regardless of the handicap. A handicapped person may have numerous personality problems or none at all.

We tend to conceptualize handicapped people as 'the blind' or 'the mentally handicapped' but within these groups there is a complete range of individual differences in family situation, life experience and adjustment. Although it is convenient to think of people as being part of a single handicap group, we should remember that, in fact, handicaps are not always single and not always simple in their effects.

Multiple handicap

We tend to classify the handicapped in separate groups. Most special schools are based on one handicap, schools for the blind, the deaf and so on, though a few are designed for doubly handicapped children. Voluntary organizations focus on one handicap, and residential provisions and clinics are similarly categorized. It is, however, not uncommon for a person to have more than one handicap. Reference to surveys where selected groups have been studied suggests that the incidence of multiple handicap is fairly high.

Sheila Hewett (1970), in her study of 180 children with cerebral palsy, found that half of the children were also mentally handicapped or suspected of being so. Sixty-three were actually confirmed as being mentally handicapped and half of these were amongst the children who had the most severe physical handicaps. In addition, more of the children who were mentally handicapped had fits than did those who were not mentally handicapped.

Another study of a group of children, in this case 200 children between the ages of two and twenty who were admitted to a hospital in France for the mentally retarded, illustrates the point. All these children were mentally retarded, 25 per cent had in addition the sensory disturbances of hearing loss and visual problems and 50 per cent had epilepsy.

An epidemiological study undertaken in the Isle of Wight (Rutter *et al.* 1970) looked at the overlap of handicaps in nine-to eleven-year-old children. They found that putting together intellectual, educational, psychiatric and physical handicaps a quarter of the handicapped children had more than one handicap. 90 per cent of the intellectually retarded children had other handicaps; four in every five had an educational handicap in that they were educationally retarded, one-third had a physical handicap and over a fifth had a psychiatric handicap. Twenty-nine per cent of the physically handicapped had another handicap, though the majority did not. Nearly a fifth had an educational handicap and one in six a psychiatric disorder. Again, one in every six was intellectually retarded.

So a significant number of handicapped people have more than one handicap and consequently more areas of behaviour are affected.

Some instances of multiple handicap can be particularly difficult to diagnose. For example, a person with cerebral palsy may also have a hearing loss but his slow reactions or lack of response to sound may be attributed to the cerebral palsy. Involuntary turning of the head may be interpreted as a search for sound sources, lack of speech and lack of response to verbal requests may be thought to be due to motor difficulties rather than to inability to hear. Only careful assessment techniques can demonstrate the extent of his problems and some time may elapse before his actual condition is understood.

On the other hand, cases have been recorded where a child has appeared to have more handicaps than he really has. For example, in the early years, a blind child with cerebral palsy may have very few responses and appear to be mentally retarded too, but later in life, when he has received a good deal of stimulation and learned how to react to his surroundings, he may prove to be much more intelligent than was first thought.

Multiple handicap can be particularly difficult for parents to accept and it is not unusual for all problems to be attributed to one handicap, particularly if mental retardation is involved. In the early years, it is more tolerable for a parent to feel that if the child could walk, or hear or were not emotionally withdrawn, he would be quite normal. To accept the extra burden of recognizing a mental limitation, in addition to cerebral palsy or deafness or autism, can be a difficult process.

Secondary handicap

In the case where a person has only one handicap, we have to consider whether he also has secondary handicaps. Any handicap is likely to create limitations which further restrict behaviour, either directly or indirectly, and one of the basic aims of early training and education is to try and avoid these. For example, a child with cerebral palsy has inadequate control of his legs and arms. This means that he has difficulty in handling toys which are suitable for his age and has fewer opportunities to move around and explore his surroundings. He has fewer experiences than non-handicapped children of the same age and fewer opportunities for learning and so is likely to have slower mental development. He remains physically dependent for longer than normal so may remain emotionally immature as he has to interact with others in the same way as a younger child, crying or shouting for assistance instead of being able to help himself. Further, the attitudes of those around him may retard his general development as it is difficult to treat an immobile, physically limited child in the same way as a mobile child of the same age.

In a similar way, a person who is mentally retarded might be kept at home by a family who feel he should be protected. He may be shielded from contact with other people, not encouraged to do anything for himself and treated as quite helpless. He then risks developing a secondary social handicap, both in daily living skills and social interaction, and may develop a behaviour problem secondary to the mental handicap through boredom and lack of firm handling.

Cultural contexts of handicap

Whether a particular condition is considered a handicap will vary with the surroundings a person lives in, with his personal situation at the time and his society's attitude towards him. A child in a family where there are other handicapped people will tend not to be seen as particularly deviant, for example if more of the children are mentally handicapped or other members of the family have fits. On the other hand, a comparatively mild handicap can be seen as a major disability in a family unfamiliar with that disability. People with the same handicap will vary in whether they regard themselves as disabled and sometimes will vary in that they regard themselves as handicapped at some times and not others.

A handicap must always be seen in terms of society and society becomes relevant from the moment of the child's birth, when friends and relatives, on hearing the news, do not send the usual congratulation cards and gifts, or from when the handicap is realized and the parents have to deal with letting other people know of the diagnosis and cope with the curiosity of friends who have noticed that the child is not developing

13

quite normally. Society is not just a background against which a handicapped person lives, but is a force which shapes his life. He will be affected by other people's behaviour, their willingness to help him or to reject him. He will be affected by the norms and values of the society he lives in; whether his community places high value on material success, sporting attainment, intellectual achievement and whether tolerance and good neighbourliness are considered important. He will be affected by the institutions and services created by his society; whether help is available to help him to lead a full life, whether provisions are made in the expectation that he will need to be removed from the community, whether organizations are available to help him and to give support to his family.

In general, any condition becomes a handicap if it causes a problem either to the person with the condition or to the people he lives with in his immediate family or in the wider community.

It has been found that the likelihood of a person being designated as handicapped is affected by the culture in which he lives. In a fast-moving, highly industrialized, competitive setting, inability to cope is more likely to becomes obvious than in less demanding surroundings, so more people are likely to be seen as handicapped in an urban area than a rural one. A handicapped person may find it easier to wander round a village where there is little danger from traffic, where there is less need to travel around, and where people are not in too much of a hurry to cope with his slower pace. Nevertheless the existence of such a person in a village community is not always as well tolerated and idyllic as is sometimes thought, as a certain amount of teasing and abuse often occurs. The prevailing availability of employment has also been found to influence the prevalence of handicap; in times of high unemployment the less able are likely to find it harder to get work and become categorized as in need of help.

The more immediate environment is relevant too. The kind of family a person belongs to, its attitudes and expectations and the degree of support it can give him will affect the likelihood of his being considered handicapped. Physical weakness may be less important in a family uninterested in sports or active pursuits but may become a handicap if it means exclusion from much family activity. A mildly mentally handicapped person may be unnoticeable in a family who are of low intelligence and have few academic interests; in this context he is unlikely to be considered handicapped. A person with the same degree of handicap in a highly intelligent family where academic success is expected is likely to be at a disadvantage.

A third consideration is the person's age and stage of life. Some conditions are seen as a handicap at some times and not at others. There are crisis points in the life of a handicapped person, which in general reflect difficult times for the non-handicapped. Starting school can be a time when a handicap becomes fully obvious for the first time as he then has to compete with his age group; adolescence too can highlight a handicap as the teenager becomes aware of his physical attractiveness and desirability as a sexual partner. It is known that in the case of mild mental handicap, reported incidence figures are higher between ten and twenty years than for the older age groups. We can assume, then, that more teenagers need to be regarded as handicapped than do adults. Various explanations for this phenomena have been suggested, which include prolonged learning—that the mildly mentally handicapped person learns more slowly but reaches an adequate level of social learning in adulthood, slower rate of maturation, or a camouflage effect—that in adulthood it is easier to find a way of life where deficiencies pass unnoticed whereas teenagers are first competing in school and then competing for and learning to do jobs.

There appear to be sex differences too in the incidence of handicap. There is a slight tendency for boys to be more likely to be considered as handicapped than girls, and it is generally considered that it is easier for families to accept that a girl stays at home, living a protected life, than it is to accept that a boy does so. A girl is more likely to help with housework, sew or knit and not be so obviously unoccupied.

A final cultural influence on a handicapped person's experience is what is generally expected to happen to him. The arrival of a handicapped person in a society can be seen as a breakdown in the expectations of that society. Most social groups have an expected life pattern and expectations of how its members will behave. A handicap makes many of the predictions irrelevant and the degree to which any group can readjust is variable. The decision which will most influence the handicapped person is whether he will be included or excluded and this in turn will depend on what is expected of him. The extreme form of exclusion is the attitude that the child should be 'put away' as early as possible, as he will not be able to share the things that his social group feels important and will not be able to contribute to his society. At the present time, a child who is seen as mentally handicapped is considered most in need of an institution where he can live a separate life; the realization of normal intelligence, however extensive the physical handicap, seems to produce an attitude against segregation and is one of the major influences on a decision to keep the child in his home. Individual communities still vary in their acceptance or rejection of the handicapped though there is evidence of a change in attitude towards acceptance over the past years. Current social attitudes are moving towards making provision for the handicapped to live within the community rather than to be segregated.

Why study handicap?

There are three basic purposes in the psychological study of handicap:

1 We need to know what are the effects of various kinds of handicap on the person with the handicap; how it affects his mental development, his progress in school, his personality, his social behaviour, his emotional reactions and his adjustment to work and the demands of life as an adult in the community.

We need to know what are the effects on a family of having a handicapped member, and how the lives of his parents and siblings are influenced.

We need to know how the non-handicapped react to the handicapped, what determines positive or negative attitudes.

2 This information should be as accurate as possible. Many books written on the subject of handicap, including those written by handicapped people, contain revealing comments on reactions to handicap. What is not always known is whether any particular experience is unique to a few individuals or common to many. For this purpose, surveys of groups of people are particularly useful as we can then learn whether any particular comment is typical of five per cent of a group or ninety-five per cent.

Much use is made, in this context, of interviews, particularly when mothers of the handicapped are being studied. The interviewer usually has an outline of the areas of information he wishes to gather but within each subject encourages the mother to talk freely. Some of the information gathered in this way is retrospective and it is not usually possible to know how reliable the mother's memory is. It is known, for example, that when looking back on how they brought up their children, mothers' recollections may become slightly distorted in the direction of what is at the time considered to be good child care practice: for example, a mother who kept to a rigid time-schedule when feeding her baby, at a time when demand feeding is popular, is likely to recall that she was less rigid than she really was. For this reason, information obtained about the present or recent past tends to be more reliable. There is also the possibility that mothers will not like to admit to an interviewer that they used methods which they feel other people might see as undesirable, such as physical punishment, using pacifiers, going out and leaving the child alone. However, the interview method is most likely to be acceptable to mothers as they can relax and chat and there are opportunities for completely new information to be revealed that the interviewer had not expected. When all the interviews are completed, the researcher can then tabulate all the views given and produce frequencies of attitude.

Research on attitudes tends to make use of questionnaires designed to discover at which point along a continuum the respondent's attitude lies; this may be an adjustment/maladjustment continuum, positive/negative attitude to the disabled, or interest/disinterest in the study of handicap.

Measures of development are used to describe particular groups. These may be tests or developmental scales which give a guide to the stages of normal development and the ages at which each occur.

When we have accurate measures of the group of people we are studying we can then look for interrelated factors in an attempt to discover what might cause change.

3 The aims mentioned above have as a basic purpose to know if we can cause changes which will make the experience of the handicapped happier, perhaps by better training and education, by providing more counselling and advice services, by giving more help and guidance to parents in helping their children to develop.

We need to know too if we can ameliorate some of the undesirable effects of handicap by changing public attitudes and by increasing the opportunities available to the handicapped.

2
Psychological effects of handicap

The development of the self-concept

All of a child's experiences during the early years contribute to his knowledge of himself. (See C3.) The foundations of the self-concept are laid during the early months when the baby begins to distinguish what is 'self' and what is 'not self' through moving and watching his limbs, learning to grasp objects, finding that he can affect his surroundings by his own movements. As he learns that objects and people are permanent and have separate existences, he names them, asks for them and pleases his parents by describing them. He learns to recognize familiar people, to know himself in a mirror and that he can influence others' behaviour and they influence his. As he goes out of the home, he learns about the world around him and later hears stories from books, radio and television of what children like himself are doing.

Any, if not all, of these experiences are less accessible to the handicapped child and it is almost always found that a handicapped child's development is slower, to a greater or lesser extent, than that of a normal child, even though the handicapped child is of normal intelligence.

Early Sensori-motor development – when the child co-ordinates his limbs, eyes and ears – is retarded by physical limitations or sensory deficits, and frustration at not being able to achieve what he wants can have an additional slowing effect. So his concept of himself, as a separate entity, is more difficult to achieve from the beginning.

Later, development of speech is more difficult. He may have

18

communication problems himself, a hearing loss or speech so poorly pronounced that his parents do not recognize it and are less likely to reward his efforts. It has been found, too, that handicapped children, particularly the mentally handicapped, are less likely to be spoken to as less is expected of them – they seem unlikely to understand or they are less responsive and show little recognition of being talked to. Being given a name and being addressed by it is a basic part of the development of a concept of oneself, and young children use their own name before using 'I' to refer to themselves. Again, if a handicapped child is spoken to less often, he is less familiar with his name.

Use of mirrors, which is generally an accepted part of the experience of a normal child, can be a difficult decision for the mother of a handicapped one as she may feel that she wishes to protect him. Mothers of children with physical disabilities may be reluctant to use mirror play.

When the child begins to listen to stories and watch television, he hears and sees accounts of children's activities which he may never have experienced and therefore has much more difficulty in identifying with the characters because he cannot imagine himself doing what they are doing.

In these activities and many more, then, the handicapped child risks being at a disadvantage. For these reasons, the most successful early training programmes have been those which brought the handicapped child's experiences as close to those of the normal child as possible, by using adapted toys he can cope with, by encouraging mothers to speak to the child as often as possible – even though response is slower, by providing trolleys, bicycles, walking frames for the less mobile child to experience movement and exploration. Scales of normal child development can be used both to assess progress and to suggest what experiences should be provided at any particular stage. (e.g. Stephen and Robertson 1972.)

Self-concept is usually inferred from what a person says about himself. If, however, he is too young or too disabled, it is necessary to observe his behaviour to see if he behaves as if, for example, he has control over his environment.

A related concept to that of the self is that of body image, which refers to a person's mental representation of his own body. This again is more difficult for the handicapped child to develop both because he has fewer experiences of using his own body and because he cannot learn as much from others about himself. Two aspects of body image are usually included

19

– what a person considers to be an ideal or desired image and what he sees as his actual body. A tendency has been noted for handicapped children to feel that the non-handicapped are perfect and there is a risk that their ideal body image will be totally different from what they see as themselves. Although a small discrepancy between the two is normal, too great a difference is generally considered psychologically maladjusted.

Realization of handicap

As the handicapped child develops a concept of himself, this concept must at some stage include the handicap. It is, however, difficult to generalize as to when this occurs, as interviews with mothers suggest that there is rarely any clear point of realization. With a congenital handicap, a child usually realizes he has a limitation at the same stage that he realizes others do not have one, perhaps when he becomes aware that other children are running and he is not.

In some cases, realization can be quite late. It is possible for a family to protect a child through the early years from knowing that his experience is different. If a child attends a residential school where everyone has the same handicap, he may not be fully aware that he is unusual. However, it is rarely possible for a handicapped person to fail to appreciate the impact of his handicap beyond adolescence. Looking for a job and dating experiences have been considered as the time when the reality of the handicap and others' attitudes towards it are fully appreciated. An exception to this is the case of the severely mentally handicapped where, because of the nature of the limitations, the handicap is often not realized at all.

Exposure to other people with the same handicap is generally an important experience with a variable effect. To generalize, children tend to find it reassuring that there are other children who have the same problems and that they are not unique. In adults, the effect is variable – some find it reassuring and relaxing to be with people who have the same problems and with whom they can share activities. Others, particularly if their handicap is of intermediate severity, will be depressed and even horrified that they are expected to be part of a handicapped group and will avoid association with the group.

A handicap acquired later in life involves a somewhat different kind of realization, in general much more rapid than the realization of congenital handicap. In this case, the self-concept has to be altered and with severe disability a totally new one has to be acquired. Alongside this process, others who knew him before he became handicapped need to get to know him again. People in the position of becoming handicapped in later life generally report that interaction is easier with new acquaintances than with those who were known previous to the handicap.

An important element in a person's self-concept is his perception of roles he can play towards others and his perception of the roles they might wish to play towards him. He may see himself as an organizer, as a provider for his family, as an entertainer at social gatherings. He may feel that others see him as an adviser, as someone who helps when problems arise, that his children see him as a powerful person. Much reappraisal of the self-concept is necessary when a handicap occurs. He needs to reshape his perception of himself and of what he sees as others' perception of him. If his concept of himself is too different from the way that others actually see him, he is likely to become maladjusted to his new situation.

The 'sick role' is often mentioned in this context. Being sick, handicapped or disabled involves playing a particular part in relation to other people, and expecting others to perform roles appropriate to a sick person. This usually involves expecting to be looked after, absolved of responsibility, and acquiesced to. Playing a sick role is necessary at times, and usual in the early stages of disability, but can cause problems within a family if it continues for too long or beyond the time when it is necessary.

Reaction to handicap acquired in adulthood is not proportionately related to the objective severity of the handicap. A comparatively mild handicap can cause a severe emotional reaction and a more severe handicap much less reaction. The causal factors in the degree of reaction seem to be what the acquired handicap means to the person in terms of his life style, his job and his interests. Acquired deafness is likely to shock a person who loves music, works as a telephone operator and spends a great deal of time in company with others, more than someone who relies less on hearing. Physical deformity is more difficult to adjust to for a person who has always cared about his appearance than for someone to whom appearance is less important.

A series of recognizable reactions have been noted in people who acquire handicaps, all of which are normal and natural

21

to some extent but can cause problems if they are excessive or last too long. Denial may occur, a refusal to accept that anything is wrong: this is seen as the individual's way of unconsciously protecting himself from a too sudden shock, and has been noted particularly in cases where the handicap is acquired suddenly.

Anxiety and depression frequently occur as reactions to the loss of former self and some former skills. Other reactions also generally felt to occur – largely at an unconscious level without the person being fully aware of what is happening – are regression, where the person behaves like someone younger, perhaps becoming overdependent; increased egocentricity, when he becomes demanding and intolerant of others' needs when they conflict with his own; withdrawal from contact with other people; increased use of fantasy, again, as an escape from facing the reality of the handicap; projection, where his feelings of inadequacy are deflected onto others and reversed so he sees others as regarding him as inadequate; new identifications, such as buying expensive possessions, or joining groups felt to be of high status to restore his damaged confidence by new and impressive associations. None of these reactions are inevitable and no person is likely to show them all. However, it is usual for some degree of a few of these reactions to be noticed.

On the whole, realization is most likely to occur at crisis points. The concept of crisis points appears frequently in the literature on handicap. These are stages which are important in normal development but are of intensified importance for the handicapped person. For him they are seen as stages where his handicap causes extra difficulties and are usually decision points as to whether he can be part of normal society or whether he plays the different role of the handicapped. Crisis points are times like going to school – either normal or special school, being accepted as a date by other boys or girls, getting a normal job and being accepted without qualification by an employer or needing sheltered work, being able to leave home and live independently and getting married and coping with a home.

These stages are made more difficult for the handicapped person because of the difficulties of knowing what to expect and inability to predict. Most non-handicapped people grow up with fairly clear expectations based on what happens to the majority of people they know. They can formulate norms on the basis of what the average person around them does and can plan careers. Handicapped people have few if any norms to guide them. Whereas the mother of a normal child can fairly confidently say to her child, 'When you go to school . . .' or 'When you have children of your own . . .', the mother of a handicapped child is hesitant in using phrases like these as she can rarely judge what his future will be.

The same uncertainties affect the handicapped person as he grows up.

Some effects in school children

Use of concepts

Self-concept and concepts of others are certainly affected by intelligence level, and it has generally been found that children with lower intelligence are less aware of themselves and other people in that they use fewer categories of description, whereas more intelligent children will be aware of differences between people in a wide range of characteristics.

Wooster (1970) compared the use of concepts of other people by boys from a school for the educationally subnormal and boys from a secondary modern school. Sixteen boys from each school were assessed. They were shown eight photographs of boys and asked to list them in order for various characteristics, such as 'most kind', 'being a bully', 'trust-worthy', 'not doing as he is told'. The ESN schoolboys, who were of limited intelligence, used all the characteristics as if they were part of the same concept. They appeared not to appreciate finer differences – the person who was seen as kind was also seen as not being a bully, as trust-worthy, as doing as he was told and so on. The Secondary Modern school boys who were of normal intelligence were much more inclined to use the concepts individually so that the photograph which ranked first on one concept might be given a middle ranking on a second and different rankings on the others.

Levels of expectation

There is disagreement as to whether being handicapped produces a low expectation of one's achievements or a high one. It has been suggested that an important personality dimension amongst the handicapped may be the success-seeking or failure-avoiding dimension. Some children appear to aim at success and not be too upset at failure, others will

23

try to avoid failure at all costs, not being concerned if they have few successes. It is thought that there is a tendency amongst the handicapped to aim at failure-avoiding as they often have a long history of failure. This would suggest that, based on past experience, their expectations would not be particularly high. However, different children have different experiences and the mentally retarded children described in the following study seem to have had high expectations.

Ringness (1961) studied pupils' ratings of their own achievements in school subjects and games and their popularity and compared the pupils' estimates with reality. The 40 mentally retarded children rated their achievements much more highly than did 40 average intelligence and 40 high intelligence children. When they were reassessed a year later, the average intelligence children had become more realistic as they grew older, the high intelligence children were already realistic but the lower intelligence children still showed as much difference between expectation and reality. It seemed that their classroom atmosphere was highly accepting and encouraging but perhaps unrealistic in that sooner or later they would have to become more aware of their limitations.

It is often felt that many handicapped young people are brought up with unrealistic aspirations. It is natural for parents and teachers to be optimistic and encouraging – much early training is aimed at leading a full adult life – but the realization of a child who leaves a school where he may only have met other handicapped children that he cannot compete with non-handicapped people can be a considerable shock. He may be expecting to apply for a job but never have been out alone, caught a bus, worked out how to arrive on time, or learned to take responsibility. For this reason, training programmes for children need to include as much exposure as possible to the world that the child will eventually live in.

Handicapped adolescents are often said to be immature. This often occurs against a background of being comparatively protected. However, maturity can only be attained through learning experiences, through making mistakes, taking responsibilities and through being with people who can be used as models for behaviour.

Marginality

A basic dilemma of the handicapped person is that of which group he belongs to, whether he should identify himself with 'the handicapped' or to what extent he should consider himself part of normal society. He finds that he is a member of society but different from most other members. Hence he is often unsure where he belongs. Group affiliation is clearly affected by the severity of the handicap and it has been suggested that the severely handicapped experience less stress here, as they are clearly handicapped and have fewer opportunities of choice. The psychological position of the less severely handicapped has been referred to as 'Marginality', as they are between total disability and no disability.

Cowen and Bobrove (1966) have studied blind and partially sighted, and deaf and hard-of-hearing adolescents in France and America. On a variety of measures of adjustment, they found that the totally disabled groups, the deaf and blind, were better adjusted than the groups of partially sighted and hard-of-hearing who were marginally disabled. The totally disabled saw themselves as receiving less pity and rejection, as being more accepted, and showed less discrepancy between themselves as they would like to be and themselves as they really were.

The more possible it is for a mildly handicapped person to hide his disability, the more likely he is to have anxieties in social situations; for example, if prejudiced remarks are made about epilepsy, should an epileptic person object and reveal his condition, or should the hard-of-hearing person pretend to be absent-minded to cover up the fact that he missed parts of the conversation. Some handicapped people go to great lengths to cover up a disability by avoiding situations which might reveal it or by producing elaborate explanations for errors caused by it. Occasionally the marginally disabled become socially withdrawn and avoid contact with other people as they are unable to tolerate the anxiety of never knowing if a disaster situation will arise and the uncertainty of whether they will be accepted.

Privacy problems

Many physical handicaps involve a loss of privacy, particularly when the disability is severe. Functions which most people regard as private need assistance – going to the toilet, washing, bathing. Even when the person is relatively independent, finding a toilet in a strange place may require assistance for a blind person or a person in a wheelchair. Privacy tends to be encroached on in personal information areas too and the problem of whether to give information about oneself is more acute for the handicapped. A person without a handicap is normally free to divulge or withhold personal details about his way of life, his physical state or his problems. The handicapped person has to consider much more carefully whether he should give information as he needs to assess how it will be received. This is not much of a problem if he is severely affected – for example totally blind or severely spastic – as his handicap is more obvious, though even then he has to cope with curiosity and gratuitous advice, and whether to mention his condition in the hope of making others feel more at ease or avoid misunderstandings about the extent of his handicap. The mildly, less obviously handicapped person is in a particular dilemma: in every situation he has to decide, first, how likely it is that his handicap will become known, and second, what will be the consequences of the discovery.

A study of 39 employees or applicants for jobs in a large steel works who were epileptic reveals the extent to which a handicap may tend to be concealed (Jones 1965). The numbers of people not revealing epilepsy may be higher than that for other handicaps as there is probably more difficulty in being accepted for work since the employer finds it difficult to assess what the effect of a fit would be. Jones found that of the 39, only 10 people had said they were epileptic when they applied for their jobs, whereas the condition in the other 29 was revealed later, mostly because they had a fit at work. It was apparently known locally that many firms would not employ epileptics.

If a handicapped person has decided to be open about his handicap, he has to decide whether it is easier to refer to it directly in a joking or serious way, whether to encourage or discourage questions or discussion, and how to cope with unwanted advice. Occasionally a person will react by exaggerating his handicapped behaviour, by being clumsier than he need be, by appearing more hard of hearing than he is. This appears to be an attempt to avoid indecision as to whether to reveal the handicap by making it very obvious to everyone.

The recommendation usually made to people with less obvious handicaps is that it is advisable to reveal it to a select few people, such as spouse, employer and close friends, but that it is not necessary to reveal it to casual acquaintances.

Communication problems

Many handicaps impair normal communication. Hearing and speech impairments have an obvious effect and less obviously non-verbal elements of communication can be disrupted too. Initial contact with a new acquaintance can become self-conscious if one person is handicapped, as the non-impaired person is aware that he should not stare but finds it difficult not to feel he is doing so and the handicapped person is usually aware of the awkwardness. Most people make use of eye contact in the course of conversation – to emphasize questions, to indicate when they expect their listener to respond, or to show interest. (See B1 and B2.) If eye contact is physically impossible because of blindness or poor control of physical movement, the non-handicapped person may experience a feeling of discomfort and unfamiliarity. The position from which to communicate can be difficult with a person in a wheelchair; unless a convenient chair is available, the non-handicapped person must decide whether to address the top of the handicapped person's head or to crouch in a rather uncomfortable position. So in addition to any difficulties he may have in speaking and hearing, the handicapped person is frequently aware of some discomfort in those talking to him and may become frustrated as he is unable to help.

Positive effects of handicap

Not all effects of handicap are undesirable. Handicaps affect different people in different ways; some they depress, while to others they are a motivating factor and a challenge. Some handicapped people express the view that because they are handicapped they have learned to be more sympathetic and tolerant. Others react by mastering activities that would seem almost impossible and certainly difficult even for the non-handicapped, as for example physically handicapped people undertaking very long walks.

The idea that compensatory development occurs in non-handicapped areas to counterbalance losses is a traditional one; for example, the blind having extremely good hearing, the mentally retarded being very musical, children with spina bifida who cannot walk being advanced in verbal activities. The idea has been little studied scientifically and it probably applies to some people but not to all. Where the loss is sensory, it seems likely that loss of one sense means that there are fewer distractions which improves concentration through the intact senses. People with a sensory loss are thought to acquire finer discriminations in their usable senses as they are more dependent on them, having fewer clues from other sources.

Variation in effect

As with every aspect of handicap there are few common patterns of reaction. Some people have little observable reaction to their handicap, others are profoundly affected. To summarize, in childhood handicaps are most likely to have a retarding effect on some areas of development. In adults a variety of emotional reactions have been observed as different individuals come to terms with living with their handicap.

3
The environment

When we are looking at the impact of handicapped people on their surroundings we need to consider both how the handicapped person fits into his environment – whether on the same terms as a non-handicapped person or as a handicapped person; and secondly, how the environment accepts the handicapped person – whether it rejects him or whether it causes unhappiness by negative attitudes.

Adjustment to society

There are many variations in definitions of adjustment and it seems that everyone who has used the concept has used slightly different characteristics to assess it. We need specific descriptions of what we mean by 'adjustment'. For, if we wish to study what helps a person to adjust – perhaps by comparing 'well-adjusted' and 'poorly-adjusted' groups – we need to identify who is 'well adjusted'. But if we asked two researchers to rate a group of handicapped people as adjusted or not, we are likely to find a considerable amount of disagreement, as they would almost certainly have different ideas of what constituted adjustment.

When working with the handicapped, we have to be clear whether we are assessing a person's level of adjustment on the same terms as that of a normal person or as a handicapped person.

For those who should be able to fit into society on the same terms as a non-handicapped person, minimal requirements would seem to be:

1 maintaining oneself by remaining employed;
2 having somewhere to live;
3 able to look after oneself well enough to maintain a healthy, adequate diet, cleanliness and sleep enough to work properly;
4 being able to keep out of trouble;
5 not depending too much on social agencies.

We can call these aspects, practical adjustments to society.

Practical adjustment for the handicapped person seems to be

1 to have someone who is willing and able to look after him, when necessary;
2 to behave in such a way that the burden of caring for him is not too great, not being so demanding or difficult as to cause stress in those around him;
3 being willing to work and to help himself as far as he is able.

The concept of adjustment has in some studies been interpreted in a way that can be seen as personal adjustment. This use of the concept includes aspects of behaviour which are necessary for either the normal or the handicapped person to live happily. The following dimensions have generally been considered important:

Independence as far as physical and mental limitations allow: being able to cope with emergencies, knowing who to go to for help and how to contact them; not totally depending on others for entertainment but being able to occupy oneself at times; being able to make decisions when necessary rather than needing to refer back to others.

Awareness of reality to avoid impossible ambitions, such as unsuitable work, unattainable possessions or hire purchase agreements which cannot be completed; not behaving in a bizarre fashion or socially inappropriate manner; awareness of basic laws in relation to property; not marrying or having children without making adequate arrangements for the future.

Adequate interpersonal relationships to avoid extreme loneliness and to avoid rejection through being unaware of other people's reactions; not interrupting or monopolizing conversations or addressing strangers in a familiar manner; awareness of basic moral behaviour, keeping promises, not borrowing money and forgetting to repay it; awareness of acceptable and unacceptable sexual behaviour; being able to contribute to friendship as well as receiving.

Reasonable emotional maturity to avoid temper outbursts, aggression or rage reactions at being thwarted; not giving in notice, or damaging property or people if annoyed.

Ability to pursue appropriate goals to avoid frequent changes of work or lodgings for trivial reasons; knowing how to change jobs, not leaving one without planning another; having some long-term aims instead of pursuing only immediate gratification.

Studies of handicapped people where better-adjusted and poorly-adjusted people have been compared have suggested that the following personality characteristics are important:

1 The better adjusted have positive self-concepts, they have more self-esteem and more readily see themselves as making a worthwhile contribution to society.
2 They are less aggressive and less anxious than the poorly adjusted; they are less likely to be annoyed or upset by what they see as unfair treatment or tactless behaviour and are more able to tolerate uncertain or ambiguous situations where they are unsure of others' reactions to them.
3 They have less need of social approval and are more able to rely on their own judgements of whether they are doing well.

Employment

To be able to find work and to keep it is one of the most important aspects of social adjustment and there is some evidence that being employed is a good general indicator of overall adjustment. Studies on adults who are adjusting to handicap acquired in later life suggest that whether a person, on leaving hospital, returns to work is not related to how disabled he is, but that those who are working, either full or part-time, report least trouble in other areas of their lives. Those who did not seek employment seemed to be completely without aims, had little social life, did not join in recreational activities and had far more complaints about their physical state and their family life.

Apart from the practical considerations of having money to live and maintain oneself, having a job improves self-esteem, helps to prevent boredom and usually increases the amount of contact with other pople.

Handicapped people, if working, are employed in three kinds of setting:

1 Some are in open employment, in ordinary jobs, employed on terms no different from those of a non-handicapped person.

2 Some are employed in what is generally referred to as 'niche' employment. This refers to the kind of job within a normal setting which is often specially arranged for the handicapped person. It may be simple and undemanding but a useful contribution to the organization. He is often not as productive as other workers but usually the employer is a sympathetic person who wishes to help. Sometimes the job is arranged as the handicapped person's mother or father works in the organization and is able to supervise when necessary. Niche jobs are often not well paid, but may be the only possibility that the employee has of working in open employment.

3 Those who cannot cope with full employment because of mental or physical limitations can be employed in sheltered workshops. Here they can be productive at a slower pace, with their work organised to be within their capacity.

Which of these three types of employment is appropriate to any person will depend on his degree of physical handicap, his intelligence level and his social and work behaviour. The effect of the physical handicap depends largely on the operations needed to perform the work. Normal intelligence makes it likely, if other handicaps are not too great, that the person will be in open employment; severely mentally retarded people are most likely to need sheltered workshops and only a few people with IQs below 50 are fully employable under present conditions and demands. The employability of people who are mildly mentally handicapped has proved more difficult to predict. Many studies have attempted to identify factors which will tell us if a person is employable but most attempts, using factors like educational level, social class, personality, adjustment, have not been successful. The factor that seems, to date, to be most involved is that of appearance, in that it seems that a mildly mentally handicapped person of normal appearance is more likely to be employed than a person who looks odd or unusual. In practice, the most effective method of finding if a mildly handicapped person can work is for him to accept a job and see if he is successful.

The majority of the mildly mentally handicapped are, in fact, in full employment; for example a survey in Edinburgh showed that two-thirds of mildly mentally handicapped school leavers had adjusted to work.

People with epilepsy too are most likely to work in full employment. A recent study of people with epilepsy showed that three-quarters of epileptics of employable age were fully employed and unembarrassed by their condition and a further 12 per cent were employed in restricted work.

In the case of people with sensory or physical handicap, in addition to the factor of intelligence level, the availability of a suitable job is important, though there is evidence that some people with this type of handicap have to take jobs which are below their capacity.

Sheltered workshops

At the present time, most sheltered workshops do work which is sub-contracted to them from local industries or organizations. Making up boxes, packing goods, assembling work, dismantling outdated equipment, filling envelopes with brochures for mailing are typical of the kind of work undertaken. Work sometimes needs to be adapted to the special needs of the workers; frames are used for holding work steady, divided boxes or blocks with the correct number of nails in sometimes need to be used to get the correct number of items in a packet.

The aims of this kind of workshop tend to be vaguer than those of workshops whose purpose is to habilitate its trainees into open industry. In this latter situation, the workshop needs to be as similar to a normal factory as possible, with clocking-in procedures, full working hours, and normal factory discipline and supervision. The sheltered workshop, however, has very few workers who will progress to a competitive level, and aims need to be expressed in terms of the satisfaction and happiness of those attending it.

Historically, the sheltered workshop which does industrial type work has become increasingly common since the 1950s. Before then, the capacity of the severely mentally retarded person to work was not fully realized. Around that time, much research was done on methods of training retarded people and it was demonstrated that the starting point of a retarded person, when he first attempted a piece of work, had no relationship to the level of skill he could attain given suitable training, and that in some cases he could reach normal levels of achievement. This training consisted of breaking down the operation to be performed into small stages and teaching each stage separately, arranging effective incentives for working, and giving a great deal of practice (see Clarke and Clarke, 1974).

In recent years a further dimension has been added to the activities of sheltered workshops. Currently there is a feeling that although it is useful for the handicapped person to extend his skills by learning to do a variety of jobs, and to find satisfaction in being productive and successful, it is not necessary that he does this kind of work all the time. Workshops are increasingly introducing breaks in the work routine when lessons are given in simple housecraft – like making beds, laying tables, making tea, and cleaning, or in social skills – like understanding money, using a telephone or washing hair, or time is spent painting or singing or in recreational activities like football, team games or swimming.

Not every severely handicapped person is able to attend a sheltered workshop. The most disabled physically and mentally handicapped need the provision of a Special Care Unit. Current experience suggests that those with a developmental level of below eighteen months tend to be unable to cope with a workshop. A Special Care Unit is designed to care for the handicapped during the day, to develop simple skills like grasping and manipulating objects, moving around, feeding oneself, using a toilet, and to keep the person as stimulated and lively as possible.

The advantages of both sheltered workshops and Special Care Units affect both the handicapped person and his family. They allow the handicapped person to feel that he goes out to work every day as do many other people around him; they provide him with a change of environment, and prevent him from being bored at home; they offer him a range of social contacts which would often not be possible if he were at home all day. They also provide an opportunity for the workshop supervisor to assess whether he is, after all, capable of being trained to progress to open employment; and the workshops allow him to earn a small amount of money. From the family's point of view, he is away from home all day in a place where they know he is well looked after and his mother can lead a much more normal life, not being restricted by the need to look after him. Were day time care not available, requests for permanent care in institutions would be much more frequent.

34

Social skills

Although being able to perform the work required is obviously of vital importance, many other aspects of being employed are involved in successful adjustment and many handicapped people lose jobs, not because they cannot do the work, but because other aspects of behaviour are inadequate or inappropriate. Problems may arise because they fail to clock in on time, they take too many days off for unacceptable reasons – perhaps not understanding that attending a football match or going to see one's social worker should be done outside working hours. They may have difficulty in being co-operative and working as part of a team, or they are unable to accept instructions without arguing. There are other problems of adaptation or social convention which may create difficulties for the handicapped employee, though of course the un-handicapped sometimes make the same mistakes. He may sit and wait for more work materials rather than trying to ask for them; he might find it difficult to chat to fellow-workers without stopping work and may wander around talking to people in other areas; another known problem is remembering to wash or bathe frequently when doing a hot and dirty job.

A lunch time visit to a cafeteria can be a confusing experience if it is unfamiliar and a certain amount of forward planning is needed to arrive at the cash desk with the right amount of food and cutlery and enough money to pay for it.

Some handicaps can involve special problems of socially unacceptable behaviour. It has been commented that deaf people sometimes make irritating noises of which they are unaware, shuffle their feet and put down objects with a great deal of clatter which is disturbing to hearing people. Blind people may rock backwards and forwards whilst they are sitting on a chair or may produce strange facial grimaces. A cerebral palsied person may be inclined to dribble when he is concentrating, or may be clumsy. Many of these habits are unremarkable to those who are used to the handicapped person, and in many cases he will only have met during childhood sympathetic people like his family and his teachers; they may have become unaware that there is anything unusual in his behaviour. It is never possible to predict whether any group of fellow workers will accept strange behaviour or reject the person completely because of his odd ways.

Another reason for breakdown in coping with society is that of boredom. If a handicapped person goes to a residential job or lives in lodgings he may be quite contented whilst working but quite unable to occupy and entertain himself in the evenings. This is most likely to happen if he has been living in a residential school, hostel or hospital where there were always people around and a great deal of entertainment provided. People in this position need to be specifically taught how to occupy themselves and concrete suggestions should be made as to what they can do, within the limits of their budget, to find entertainment.

Employers' attitudes
Whether or not an employer will hire a person with a particular handicap for a particular job depends of course on the demands of the job and how well the employer feels that it would be done, but it appears that positive or negative attitudes are equally important. When groups of employers have been asked if they would employ people with various handicaps, very roughly half say they would and half say they wouldn't. Their answers, however, vary in relation to which handicap is being discussed. Surveys suggest that on the whole they say that they are least willing to employ a person whose handicap is mental retardation, particularly if the job applied for is a management or sales job. Those who say they would hire a mentally handicapped person – one survey quotes this figure as 20 per cent – say that they would employ him in a production job. There also tends to be resistance to hiring blind people in management, clerical or sales jobs: although some of these jobs would be inappropriate and impossible for a blind person, the employers' resistance appears partly to be due to lack of knowledge of the ways in which blind people can cope with getting around, keeping notes and compensating for lack of sight by use of other senses. Deaf people tend to be considered most acceptable in clerical jobs. Over half the employers would not hire an epileptic person for production, management or sales jobs.

The negative attitudes which appear seem to be related to the economic aspects of employment; many employers say that they feel that the extra costs which they see as being involved in hiring the handicapped are not offset by benefits. It seems that people with obvious handicaps are most likely to be employed initially because the employer has a positive and sympathetic attitude.

Luckily, there are many employers who do hire handicapped

people, and on the whole, studies indicate that where a handicapped person remains in employment, he compares favourably with his non-handicapped counterpart on performance.

Society's attitudes to handicap

Having looked at some of the ways in which handicapped people adjust to society and fit into their environment we now turn to ideas on how society regards the handicapped.

On the whole surveys of public attitudes to handicap indicate a change in a positive direction over the years, though there is still a considerable proportion of negative response. It is clear that if any community or section of a community has strongly negative attitudes to disability, this will make a handicapped person's adjustment to that society a great deal more difficult. He risks becoming withdrawn or anxious and unwilling to attempt to enter unfamiliar situations as he does not know how he will be received.

Several large-scale surveys on public attitudes to epilepsy have been carried out between 1949 and 1964. Percentages of responses indicate that during this time there was a change in a positive, accepting direction. For example, the number of people who agreed with the statement that epilepsy is not a form of insanity increased from 35 per cent to 74 per cent. Those who felt that epileptics should be employed in the same manner as everyone else increased from 45 to 75 per cent. However, at the time of the last survey there was still about a quarter of the population who were expressing negative attitudes: they agreed with statements that suggested that people with epilepsy should be excluded from normal life, and said no to questions like whether they would like their child to attend school with an epileptic child.

Studies of attitudes to the physically disabled appear just slightly less favourable and the most common finding has been that half the people interviewed had primarily negative attitudes.

On the whole, though, people who are accepting towards one handicap are more likely to be accepting towards all handicaps; it is unusual to find a person who has a positive attitude to, say, blindness and a strongly negative one to physical handicap. A rejecting attitude towards the disabled is usually found to be part of a generally prejudiced attitude towards any group seen as different, whether ethnic or religious. The person who is highly intolerant of handicap is also likely to be intolerant of people who belong to other groups, particularly minority groups, different from his own. Goffman (1963) uses the concept of 'stigma', a negative concept attached to all groups who tend to be seen as discredited, not quite human, and not eligible to be part of society. He sees stigma as attaching to anyone who does not fit in with society whether they be disabled or mentally ill, belong to a racial or ethnic minority or have a social handicap like having been in prison.

Although there is a tendency for accepting people to accept all handicaps, there seems to be a difference between physical and mental handicaps, in that physical handicaps are somewhat better accepted than mental. This may be because it is often more difficult to communicate with the mentally handicapped and there are fewer points of common interest which can be discussed. Another possible reason is that on the whole it is more difficult for a non-handicapped person to understand how it feels to be mentally handicapped than it is for him to imagine having the same mind in a different body. Everyone has experience of lowered physical efficiency at times but to imagine oneself in a position of more limited mental capacity is far more difficult.

There have been several attempts to discover if any particular section of the community is more accepting than others:

Sex difference: Studies have produced varying results but conclude either that there are no differences or that females are more accepting than males. This is seen as being consistent with what is normally found to be a female personality characteristic of being more caring about people, of wanting to be protective towards those more helpless and of being less critical of others. This finding has been repeated with adolescent girls.

Intelligence: There is no good evidence that intelligence level is related to positive or negative attitude to the disabled.

Age: Children have little reaction to disability at a preschool level as at that stage they all have limitations and are not aware enough of other people to be aware of disabilities. There is some evidence that negative attitudes to disability increase with the age of the child and are more common in secondary school children than primary. On the whole, age has little effect in adults except that there is a slight tendency for younger adults to be more accepting than older people. This finding may be simply due to the fact that attitudes have generally become more positive over the years, thus influencing the younger generation.

Education, socio-economic level and occupation: Evidence is very mixed on the relationship between attitude and these areas and few clear findings have been established. There is a suggestion that people of upper socio-economic levels are more accepting of mental and emotional handicap than of physical handicaps; they value good intelligence and emotional stability more than they value physique, and hence they are inclined to be more sympathetic towards those with a disability in this area. Another interesting suggestion is that people who have jobs where physical appearance is important are more rejecting of physical handicap than those who are in occupations where physical appearance is less important. This finding, however, appears to contradict the previous one; but further research is needed to make this relationship clearer.

On the whole, it is likely that prejudice towards handicap is spread fairly generally amongst different classes, occupation groups and people of different educational levels.

Personality: Personality characteristics which have been identified as more common in the accepting person are similar to those which characterize the well-adjusted handicapped person. They appear to have higher self-concepts, lower levels of anxiety, higher need for social approval and greater ability to tolerate ambiguity.

Situation: The situations where prejudice is most evident have been shown to vary in a way that would be expected. There is least likely to be evidence of a negative attitude in comparatively impersonal situations such as meeting a handicapped person on a train or at a lecture, or in any public place where the contact is brief, does not necessarily involve interaction and can be terminated fairly quickly. In close, personal situations, prejudice is most likely to be evident – as when a disabled person is seeking a job or looking for lodgings or is wishing to marry into a family.

Interactions of the handicapped and
non-handicapped

Many observations have been made on the social interactions of handicapped and non-handicapped people. In the less successful interactions, disabled people commonly feel that they are being treated as if they were totally disabled and incapable of any normal response at all. A deaf person may be treated as if he cannot observe anything and does not notice if he is being discussed; a physically handicapped person may be assumed to be unable to answer for himself or be shouted at as if he is unable to hear; the non-handicapped person may address another non-handicapped person present rather than the subject of the conversation – as in the classic situation where the highly intelligent, physically disabled person heard the question, 'Does he take sugar in his tea?' This kind of reaction appears to amount to an over-generalization of the handicap and a difficulty on the part of the non-handicapped in understanding what the effects of any particular disability are.

An interesting way of helping the non-handicapped to empathize with the disabled has been used with older school children. They each spent a day as a handicapped person, being blindfolded or confined to a wheelchair, and continued their normal school life. At the end of the day they had developed a much greater understanding of how a handicapped person feels.

Research has shown that in interactions with the handicapped, non-disabled persons become stereotyped in their behaviour in that they tend to repeat certain fixed patterns of acting and responding, and tend to repeat the same phrases. They become much more inhibited and over-controlled than they are in interactions with other non-handicapped people. This inhibition relates to a need felt by the non-handicapped to consider each subject of conversation carefully before they begin on it, in case the topic should be tactless or hurtful to the listener. He may feel that he should avoid references to activities in which the handicapped person may not be able to participate; not talk of going for long walks or going dancing to a wheelchair-bound person, and not refer to anything he has seen to a blind person. In practice, of course, the physically handicapped person may enjoy going for walks in his chair and enjoy watching dancing, and the blind person will normally use the concept of seeing too, in a different sense.

It has been found, also, that the non-handicapped will tend to finish conversations with the handicapped more quickly than they would with another person, as they find the activity more stressful. Further, they are less able to concentrate on what has been said and have a less accurate idea of the views that have been expressed.

Attitude change

As it seems likely that the mental health and well-being of a handicapped person will be influenced by public attitudes, it is important to discover how attitudes can be changed in a positive direction.

An attempt to change attitudes towards mental illness was undertaken by Cumming and Cumming (1957) in a small Canadian town. They held a series of group discussions, showed films over six months and assessed the attitudes of the residents before and after that period. The results indicated that change in attitude was possible as long as the ideas fitted in with currently-held views but was resisted when a strongly-held view was challenged. The participants were able to accept that the range of normal behaviour is often wider than is generally believed and that deviant behaviour has a cause and so can be understood and modified. However, they were unable to accept that normal and abnormal behaviour can be seen as occurring as part of the same continuum and are not qualitatively different. This latter reaction is generally interpreted as indicating a fear and rejection of mental illness and a denial of the possibility that anyone could become mentally ill.

Work on attitudes towards the handicapped suggests that neither information alone, nor contact with the disabled alone are sufficient in themselves to change attitudes, but that the effect of these combined has a favourable impact.

Studies of contact with the disabled in relation to attitude are either based on the reports of contact of the subjects being studied or on arranged contact sessions. In the former case, a group of people are asked if they have had any contact with the disabled. On the basis of their replies, they are divided into two groups – those who report that they have had contact and those who say they have not. The attitudes towards the handicapped in these two groups are then compared. This method is rather unsatisfactory as what the subjects mean by

41

contact is not always the same and the amount and kind of contact will vary. Results from these studies show that on the whole, people who have had contact with the disabled have slightly more favourable attitudes than those who have not, but the differences are not great and a few reports show the opposite finding, concluding that those who have had contact with the handicapped have more negative attitudes. This latter finding is probably due to the kind of contact experienced. It is known that one factor which influences reaction to contact alone, without information, is the surroundings in which the contact takes place. For example, visiting a handicapped person in hospital, if the surroundings are disturbing to the visitor, can have a negative effect.

When contact experiences are arranged and reactions studied, the general finding is still that contact alone does not change attitudes. In one project, attending a summer camp with physically disabled children had no effect on non-handicapped children. In others, children who were in school classes with mentally retarded children and with children who had had amputations did not become more positive. In fact, in the latter case, the children became more negative towards the amputees.

Similarly, providing information on disability through books, films, television and lectures increases a person's information about the handicapped but has not been shown to affect his attitude in any useful way.

In contrast, contact plus information has been shown to produce more favourable attitudes. One study was conducted at a summer camp for handicapped children. At the beginning of the camp new counsellors' attitudes were compared with those of counsellors who had worked at the camp previously and were found to be less positive. During the camp the counsellors, of course, had continuous contact with the children and were given information by the professionals on the camp staff. By the end of the camp there were clear changes in the attitudes of the new counsellors in a positive direction.

Another experiment attempted to change the attitudes of high-school girls towards the deaf-blind. Two groups of girls were chosen, a group who had the most positive attitudes and a group who had the most negative. The project involved six hours of information on the deaf-blind, instruction in the manual alphabet and opportunities to communicate with deaf-blind individuals. The students with the most positive attitudes did not change – presumably because there was little room for change as their attitudes were already positive – but the students with initial negative attitudes showed positive attitude changes: they did more voluntary work than previously and read more about deaf-blindness. Besides demonstrating that information together with contact can change attitudes, this study also suggests that with the right experiences, attitudes can be changed in a very short time.

So prejudice towards the disabled certainly exists but there is some hope, from current trends, that it will diminish in future. The increase in community care and facilities should mean that more people have contacts with the handicapped in everyday life. Together with radio and television programmes about mental health and mental handicap, we should have the necessary ingredients for attitude change. The increased involvement of volunteer workers in hospitals and in many local organizations for the handicapped can be expected to provide increasing contacts for members of the community, though it seems important, from the research findings, that they should be given supporting information too.

Environmental curiosity

Apart from the positive or negative aspects of public attitude, there is another characteristic of non-handicapped people which can cause problems for the handicapped, and particularly for mothers of handicapped children – that is, curiosity. Many people feel curious about the handicapped and wonder why he is as he is, and how he manages his everyday life. Attitudes of handicapped people to this curiosity vary; some will be quite happy to discuss their condition and may feel a sense of relief at being able to mention it, while others will resent curiosity as an intrusion. We have some information in this area on the way mothers feel. There appears to be no majority attitude to questions; various surveys show that roughly half of the mothers questioned said that they encouraged questions about the child and the other half said that they resented them and felt annoyed at being asked about an obviously different child. Clearly, the nature of the questions and the attitudes of the questioner are relevant. The majority of mothers welcome interest as long as it is genuine, sensible and not advisory; gratuitous advice and staring are not welcomed and of course tactless remarks are disliked. Sometimes a mother will escape such curiosity by deliberately avoiding contact with other people.

The problem of dealing with questions and comments from others is most acute when the child is first taken out and the mother is uncertain of what the reactions of friends and neighbours will be; later on, acquaintances are more likely to know about the handicap, and the parents become more adept at coping.

The terminology of handicap

From time to time, the terminology used in relation to the handicapped undergoes change. This is usually either because the term is felt to be no longer appropriate or because it has acquired a derogatory connotation. The phrase 'deaf and dumb' is now rarely used as it is realized that most deaf people are capable of some speech, and certainly make expressive sounds; 'hearing impaired' is now much more acceptable and emphasizes the fact that there are degrees of deafness. The name 'mongol' is beginning to disappear as it is felt that despite the superficial facial resemblance which originally produced the term – when Langdon Down, a hundred years ago, thought that the mentally handicapped could be classified into racial types – these people are totally unconnected with the Mongol race. The name 'Down's Syndrome' or 'Down's Disease' is gradually being substituted.

Words which become stigmatized are largely connected with mental illness and mental handicap: the terms 'moron', 'imbecile', 'idiot', 'lunatic', gradually became terms of abuse and have been replaced by more acceptable terminologies, like 'mentally handicapped' or 'mentally ill'. In the field of physical handicap the term 'cripple' is no longer liked; 'disabled' or 'physically handicapped' is preferred.

These changes tend to occur through pressure from professional groups who feel that the undesirable attachments to words have become too great, but usage of the older terms tends to continue, particularly amongst those with more negative attitudes.

Attitudes of professionals

One particular group of people in society who have an important influence on the attitudes and experiences of the

44

handicapped are those who are professionally involved Doctors, nurses, health visitors, social workers all have contact with the handicapped from time to time, and their reactions vary. Surveys of the experiences of handicapped people and mothers of the handicapped find that at one extreme, some are entirely satisfied with the help they have been given, whilst at the other extreme, some may feel that they have had no help at all and have had to cope with their problems alone. Where professional help has been found inadequate several reasons have been suggested. Not all professional groups have had adequate training in dealing with the problems of the handicapped and they may feel unsure of how to help the mother to cope with problems and how to answer the questions that arise. In some cases, frequent contact with the handicapped has had the effect that the professional has forgotten the impact of the handicap on the individual who has had only one experience; he may feel the individual is over-reacting to a minor handicap since he knows so many people who are far more handicapped. Finally, it seems that a professional person may seem unhelpful because he is embarrassed and frustrated at not being able to contribute anything which seems to him to be practically useful.

However, from the handicapped person's point of view, and particularly from a mother's point of view, although practical help is valued, a sympathetic and helpful attitude is of equal importance. Even if intentions to give practical help are ineffective, time spent listening to problems and giving reassurance is clearly appreciated.

4
Families of the handicapped

Initial reactions to the child's handicap

Handicaps occur at different times of life and become obvious at different times. In some cases, the person is born with a handicap, as in most cases of cerebral palsy or mental handicap. Others are acquired later through accident or illness. When a child is born with a handicap, it is not always obvious at birth. Most cases of Down's Syndrome or physical deformity are recognized when the child is born but many handicaps become obvious only when the child fails to develop usual behaviours. The parents may not realize that anything is wrong until he fails to walk when other children of the same age are walking or until they notice that compared with a neighbour's child he is far less responsive. If the child is a first child and there are no other children around for comparison, the parents may not realize for some time that the child is not developing normally. So the time of recognition of a congenital handicap depends on the expected time for each milestone.

The immediate psychological effects of a child's handicap on his parents will tend to vary according to when and how suddenly they recognized his condition.

Few, if any, parents expect a handicapped child. In the rare cases where the possibility of a handicap could theoretically have been known by the mother before the birth, in practice it seems not to be considered. A Canadian report of interviews with mothers of children with thalidomide-induced limb deficiency suggested that mothers had not accepted the possibility of damage to the child, though the effects of thalidomide had become known during their pregnancy (Roskies 1972).

In virtually every case the parents will have hopes and expectations of the child before he is born. Almost every new mother asks two questions after delivery – 'Is it a boy or a girl?' and 'Is it all right?' If the response to the second question is 'No' or an evasion, the adjustment to having a handicapped child begins at that point.

In this situation, where knowledge of the handicap is sudden, fairly clear reaction patterns have been observed. The first response is shock and a feeling of disbelief that this could happen. This is followed by a desire to be left alone whilst the mother comes to terms with the news. This phase is typically followed by a mourning reaction which is seen as grief for the perfect child that had been expected.

Much is written concerning the best way to break the news to the mother that her child has a handicap. Most information is gained through later interviews with mothers asking them to look back on their experiences and evaluate them. We know that there is a tremendous variation in who tells the parents – it may be a doctor, nurse or midwife. Sometimes the father is told first and he tells the mother. Some parents are told gradually by minimizing the severity of the handicap at first and later revealing its extent, others are given all the information at once. Some mothers are shown the baby straight away, others are discouraged from seeing the baby for a while. It is difficult to be sure which way is best as usually each parent has only one experience and is unable to compare with other possible experiences. However, we know that the majority of mothers who have definite views express a preference for openness, honesty and full information. Evasions and half-truths are rarely effective and can lead the mother to feel the situation is worse than it is. Many mothers also express indignation that information which they have a right to know should be held back.

When the handicap is not obvious at birth, the process of realization is more gradual and there are individual variations in the rate at which parents can come to accept the child's handicap. Many emotional reactions have been described. Inspection of the literature produces a considerable list of feelings which have been observed in and reported by parents: depression, feelings of isolation, shock, frustration, anger; guilt at the possibility that the handicap might have been caused

47

by something the mother did in the past; harsh criticism of the doctors or nurses involved at the birth, or of any authority which is seen as unsympathetic and unhelpful; fright and horror at wishes that the child will die (although this kind of feeling is difficult for a parent to express, it is not particularly unusual either in the early stages or when the child and parents are all older and the parents begin to wonder what will happen to him when they die); loss of self-esteem at feeling themselves unable to produce a normal child, and defeat.

No parent is likely to experience all these reactions; some may not experience any noticeable pattern of response, and it should not be regarded as inevitable for any parent to have these feelings. We have little idea about how common any of these reaction patterns are, but for any single identifiable reaction it seems likely that it will be a major problem for a few, and may or may not be realistically based.

To illustrate a group of mothers in the East Midlands (Hewett 1970) who had children with cerebral palsy were asked during interviews if they felt isolated. For most of the 21 per cent who said they did feel isolated, the experience seemed to be a feeling rather than real isolation as they were not noticeably cut off from social contacts. Clearly for these mothers it was possible to feel isolated without actually being so. On the other hand some mothers had little social contact and might have been expected to feel isolated but they did not. So in terms of numbers, a minority of these mothers felt isolated. However, for those who did, isolation could be a considerable problem. Mothers who have little contact with others in the same position tend to wonder if anyone else feels the same as they do, and have many doubts about whether they are handling the child in the right way. There is a definite risk of isolation if the child is difficult to take out, the family has no car, and if they live in an isolated setting.

A frequently mentioned reaction to learning that a child is handicapped is that of 'shopping around'. Parents may visit several doctors, often privately, consult various societies, organizations and perhaps faith healers in a search to find a cure for the condition. This reaction is in fact comparatively rare. In the East Midlands study mentioned above, mothers were asked if they had consulted anyone else besides their original doctor. Eighty per cent had never asked for advice outside the National Health Service and only three of the remaining thirty-six mothers had sought more than one kind of private help. Similar results have been found in other studies of parents of handicapped children and it is generally found that 80 per cent do not seek an opinion beyond the first.

Rearing a handicapped child

Undoubtedly, rearing a handicapped child is likely to involve extra anxieties and problems for the parents. However, it is necessary to remember that raising a normal baby can also be an anxious process for many mothers, and a certain degree of anxiety is expected in any mother. It is often fruitful to compare mothers of handicapped children with mothers of normal children in the same social setting; only then is it possible to assess the additional problems of having a handicapped child.

In general, as a handicapped child grows up, although his mother may have been initially very aware of his handicap he becomes accepted more and more as a normal child in that the aspects of his normality become more important. When the handicap is obvious at birth, mothers tend to report that they began to accept the child when they looked into his eyes and saw how normal he looked. This eye contact seems to be the beginning of a mother–child attachment. From then, it is the normal aspects of the child which are important to the mother, and each milestone he achieves on the scale of normal development is welcomed. Investigations of methods of rearing handicapped children have shown in general that most mothers bring up their handicapped children in the same way as they bring up their normal children, with allowances made for the slower pace of development.

Decision problems

The fact of the child's handicap will usually make more decisions necessary than would be the case with a normal child, and in many cases it is difficult to decide what is best for the child. Many decisions are not always clear and some disadvantages can be involved whatever choice is made. For example, if a child has a handicap which needs admissions to hospital for surgery during childhood, the choice will have to be made between his having the operations for the sake of his physical adaptation and accepting any emotional reaction he may have from being away from home and perhaps suffering pain or discomfort; or not sending him to hospital whilst he is very young for the sake of his emotional well-being. Neither of these seems obviously right or wrong. As he is developing, a decision of principle often has to be made of whether to insist on his performing all activities in a normal way, so that he will be less obviously different when he is older, or to allow him to operate in whatever way he finds easiest for the sake of maximizing his experiences. Mothers of children with limb deficiency due to thalidomide sometimes had to make this decision, as occasionally a child could use his feet more comfortably than his hands and would have found more satisfaction in using his feet to grasp though this would tend to emphasize his abnormality. A similar situation is that of the deaf child; many deaf children appear to find it easier to use signs to communicate and a decision has to be taken either to encourage this, or discourage it so as to increase the likelihood that he will use normal speech to communicate.

As the handicapped child grows up he will have a pattern of abilities; some things he will do well, other activities will be very difficult for him – for example he may be good at drawing and spend a great deal of time producing pictures, but very poor at ball games. Decisions have to be made as to whether to allow him to spend as much time as he likes drawing, so encouraging him to develop his highest abilities, or whether to insist that he tries to achieve what he is not good at and play ball games with him to try to remedy his deficits. A compromise is usually necessary here, and it is sometimes found that being allowed to do the activity he likes can be used as a reward for an attempt to do something difficult for him.

One of the biggest decisions a parent of a handicapped person tends to make is that of whether it is possible to look after him at home or whether he should go into permanent residential care. With a young child, most people agree that he is happiest at home, although conditions sometimes make it impossible for him to stay; we shall discuss reasons for needing permanent care in Chapter 9. For an older child or adult the decision becomes more difficult, as there are advantages in going away from home just as there are advantages in a normal child going to boarding school. He will have more companionship, a wider range of training facilities, and he will learn to be more independent. There are likely to be more entertainments provided than is possible at home, and life in a residential institution, whether it be school, hospital or hostel, is geared towards his needs. On the other hand, he is likely to have less personal attention than at home, and may feel that he is being rejected from the family. Parents of severely mentally and physically handicapped children tend to feel that at some stage the child will need residential care and they accept this as long as it is for the child's own good. It can be reassuring for a parent to know that there are facilities for the child to be looked after should they no longer be able to care for him, perhaps because he becomes too heavy for them to handle, or too difficult in behaviour, or they become ill or too old. Some hospitals have a long-term waiting list so that the parent has the reassurance that the hospital knows their child and a place will be available for him some time in the future in case it is needed. As would be expected, parents' attitude towards their children going into permanent residential care are very much affected by what they know of the facilities available and how they regard the quality of these facilities.

There is sometimes an implication in studies of the handicapped that there is a theoretical 'ideal' set of circumstances in which a handicapped child could live and be brought up; that he could be totally accepted and not overprotected, develop his maximum potential in all areas and avoid developing any behaviour problems or personality disorders. Although this is obviously a desirable goal, actually to define the concepts involved is difficult. Because decisions have to be made which inevitably involve some loss of possible advantages, it is impossible to generalize as to what an ideal upbringing for a handicapped child could be; much depends on the individual child, his particular family and the services available to them.

Parents' priorities and predictions

We know a little of the way in which parents of handicapped children regard their futures. When the child is of pre-school age, the kind of school he will go to is seen as being of major importance. Whether he will be accepted in a normal school or whether he will need a special school is seen as a symbol of whether he will be accepted as part of the normal world.

Again looking forward, adolescence is seen as a critical time, as it is another period when normality is tested and the handicapped person may or may not be accepted by his non-handicapped peers on equal terms. In general, when the child is young, parents would prefer that as he grows up he will associate with the non-handicapped rather than people of his

51

own handicap group, although if the child is severely handicapped this is seen as unlikely to be possible. Adolescence, however, is the time when parents are most likely to feel that association with other handicapped adolescents may be beneficial to their child. Whether future marriage for the child is predicted depends on the degree of handicap. Mothers of girls with limb deficiencies (Roskies 1972) tended to foresee a rather protected marriage relationship for them.

In fact, of course, parents of handicapped children are less likely to be able to predict a future for their children than are parents of normal children. In many cases, they have little acquaintance with other, older people with the same handicap, and if they have it is difficult to compare handicaps. Thus they have no standards by which to judge the future and the lack of being able to predict what can be expected can produce extra anxieties.

Acceptance or rejection

These are commonly used concepts in the study of handicap but not always easy to apply to a particular situation. The usual implication, of course, is that acceptance is a good thing and rejection a bad one. Literal physical rejection is in most cases obviously not in the child's best interests, but is, however, comparatively rare. For example, Halliday *et al.* (1965) studied 95 children with spina bifida who survived initial surgical treatment of their condition following birth, and found that only five went to permanent institutions and that four of these were illegitimate, so may not in any case have been kept by their mothers.

When the child remains within the family, although he has literally been accepted in a physical sense the concept of acceptance is more complicated. Accepting the fact that the child is handicapped is one stage, but we need to consider too whether his limitations have been accepted. Professional advisers who have been consulted are most likely to have given a realistic view of the child's future but are likely to have avoided being over-optimistic so that the parents will not become disillusioned; the parents may not have accepted the described limitations but may continue to aim at a higher developmental level for him than professional advisers would predict. It is clearly undesirable for these ambitions to be too unrealistic as this will lead to frustration for both parent and child. On the other hand, it is unhelpful for the most pessimistic view of the child to be taken. Aiming slightly higher than is strictly realistic has occasionally produced surprising results.

We should note that acceptance of the child within the family is not a once and for all event. His presence within the family may be accepted when he is small and can be regarded as a baby but it can be more difficult to accept him later. Differences between him and his brothers and sisters become more obvious, and he may have become heavy to handle physically, difficult in behaviour or upsetting to other members of the family.

It has sometimes been commented that the child's belonging to a recognized diagnostic group can make it more difficult for the family to feel that he is one of them; he sometimes appears to have more in common with other spastics or other Down's Syndrome children than he does with his brothers and sisters and his achievements and personality may be seen as related to his condition rather than to him as an individual.

Overprotection

Overprotection is another commonly used concept and is generally considered undesirable as it limits the child's development by making him less independent and slower to develop self-care skills. If he is not allowed to climb because he might fall, then he is less able to develop gross motor skills; if he is not allowed out alone in case he wanders into the road, then he will not learn to find his way around. However, in practice, the difference between protection which is necessary and overprotection is difficult to define. Many handicapped children are in reality more likely to fall if they climb, because of poorer co-ordination of limbs or fits; children of limited mental age may well be more likely to be unaware of the dangers of traffic. The description of overprotection can clearly only be used if the child is prevented from being involved in activities where the risks to his safety are very small.

Parents of handicapped children often feel that they should be more protective towards their handicapped child because of other people's attitudes. They feel that if their handicapped child had an accident, then others would think that he was neglected, that he was not really wanted and that his parents did not care about his safety because he was handicapped.

In their study of a group of families of handicapped children on the Isle of Wight. Rutter *et al.* (1970) found that there was a trend towards the proportion of families who reported problems of disorganization of routine, impairment of social relationship and of dissatisfaction with services available, to be greater when the child was most severely handicapped, though the association between numbers of problems and severity of handicap was not particularly strong. Clearly other factors were involved too.

Families with children who had physical disorders and brain dysfunction, including epilepsy, were most likely to have problems of disorganization of routine when compared with families with asthmatic children or children with a psychiatric disorder. (Physical disorder in this study refers to any disorder which is chronic – usually lasting at least a year, is associated with persistent or recurrent handicap of some kind, and was present during the year previous to the study.)

Disturbances of family relationships were reported most by parents who had children with brain dysfunction or psychiatric disorder and less by those who had children with physical disorder. Dissatisfaction with services was mentioned with equal frequency by all families.

We shall now examine some of the particular areas where families with handicapped children are felt to have problems.

Physical care of the child. One frequency count showed that the most stressful condition for the mother to cope with is incontinence which involves extra washing, extra costs for nappies or special pants, cleaning up after the child, and extra time spent changing him. Incontinence also creates difficulties in taking the child out visiting and staying away from home. The second most stress-creating condition was the child not being able to walk. This can be very tiring for the mother as she has to lift him frequently and makes it more difficult to use buses for transport as she has to take him out in a wheelchair. A third stress-producing condition was the child having manifestations of brain damage; this was as stressful as the child not walking. Manifestations of brain damage include behaviour like hyperactivity, uncontrolled and disorganized activity, inability to tolerate frustration and screaming episodes.

Problems of young mothers. Younger mothers are felt to have particular difficulties with a handicapped child, particularly if it is the first child. Some handicaps are more common in children of younger mothers, for example the mothers of children with spina bifida are younger as a group than average. In this case the ordinary anxieties of looking after a young baby are increased by the uncertainties of handling a handicapped one.

Fewer benefits of parenthood. It has been said that parents of handicapped children get fewer benefits from parenthood besides having extra problems. They are rewarded less often by the child's achievements, when he begins to walk or speak. The child may sometimes be less responsive to them by smiling less readily or imitating baby talk. The parents are also less likely to find satisfaction in his achievements during the school years and later – learning to read, good exam performance, success in a career. This does not imply that there are no satisfactions in bringing up a handicapped child; in fact a sign of progress in a very slowly developing child can be welcomed in a proportionately greater way than the same achievement in a normal child, but a scaling down of values and expectations needs to occur.

Discipline. Whether and in what situations a handicapped child should be punished for undesirable behaviour has been thought to be a source of difficulty. It can seem very unfair to punish a child if he is seen as not being able to understand why he is being punished or if his misdemeanour may have been due to his handicap, for example when a physically handicapped child breaks something.

However, results from one study at least suggest that in practice discipline is rarely a big problem. Hewett (1970) found that the mothers of cerebral palsied children she interviewed had very similar views on discipline to the views of the mothers of normal four-year-olds interviewed in another study. A large majority of mothers in both groups said that they approved in general of smacking children when they misbehave. The majority (71 per cent) of the mothers of the physically handicapped said that their policy on smacking their handicapped child was the same as for their other normal children. Those who felt that smacking their child was not appropriate felt so because a mental handicap prevented the child from understanding what it meant or because the child was too young or too handicapped to be naughty in the same sense as an older, non-handicapped child. Only 5 per cent of the children in the sample were exempted from all punishment and they tended to be the most mentally and physically handicapped. Whatever the method of punishment used, 95 per cent of the mothers said that they used broadly the same methods as for their other children.

Going out with the child. Being able to take a handicapped child out easily can be a major advantage. When it is difficult to take the child out, the mother has practical difficulties – like not being able to shop, and personal difficulties in that she risks feeling isolated and restricted. Problems in taking a handicapped child out are of two kinds: either there are physical difficulties of mobility if the child cannot walk or has frequent fits, or there are problems of unpredictable, unruly behaviour, where shops and particularly supermarkets are difficult to negotiate and the mother feels embarrassed if the child behaves badly in public. In the Isle of Wight study (Rutter *et al.* 1970), parents of children with brain dysfunction seemed to have the greatest problems. Forty-one of the forty-six families with these children reported that their freedom of movement was limited by the child. Nineteen of the fifty-nine families with physically disabled children had the same problem. It has generally been found that owning a car makes taking a severely handicapped child out much easier.

Going out without the child. As would be expected from the previous paragraph, the number of children with brain dysfunction in the Isle of Wight study who could not be left alone was again fairly large; thirty-five of the forty-six families of children with brain dysfunction felt that their child could not safely be left alone at home. Fifteen of the fifty-nine families with physically disabled children had the same problem. Numerically, in the East Midlands study (Hewett 1970) the problem was smaller and only twenty of the 180 mothers interviewed felt they could not leave their child unattended, though in this case the mothers were not being asked about leaving their child for long periods. In some cases, the child could not be left either because they fell frequently or because they were mentally handicapped. The mentally handicapped child, if he was mobile, presented a big problem in this respect. In contrast,

56

some physically handicapped children were very easy to leave as long as they were securely strapped into their chairs.

In the Hewett study there was no evidence that parents went out together less often than do parents of normal children. If they did not go out, the reason was often unrelated to the handicapped child, but they simply felt, as do some parents of normal children, that a parent has a responsibility not to go out much when their children are young. Parents who wanted baby sitters did seem to find them, though they felt that it was much more difficult to find someone who they felt was capable of looking after the child, and who was willing to take the responsibility. A child who had fits was a particular problem in this context.

Care if mother hospitalized. The possibility that a mother may not be able to take care of the child for a while is a worrying one for many mothers. This could be a problem for nearly half the mothers of cerebral palsied children (Hewett 1970) if the situation arose. They were asked how they would cope if they had to be temporarily absent from home. They felt that their normal children could be looked after almost completely by the family but that only fifty-six of the 180 handicapped children could be cared for within the family or with help from friends and neighbours. This feeling seemed to be partly due to relatives lacking confidence in handling a child with cerebral palsy and partly due to mothers feeling a reluctance to ask other people to accept the extra responsibilities.

Holidays. The majority of families with handicapped children manage to take holidays but for a few, the child can make holidays difficult or impossible. Major difficulties are severe physical and mental handicaps, difficult behaviour, bedwetting and frequent fits. In the Isle of Wight study (Rutter *et al.* 1970) fourteen of the fifty-nine families with children with physical disorder and thirteen of the forty-six families with children with brain disorder found holidays a problem. Of the total group of parents interviewed, twelve had taken no holidays since they had had the child and three had done so but had had such great difficulties that they were reluctant to go again. So although difficulty in taking holidays affects a minority, it imposes limitations on those who are affected.

In the study of mothers of cerebral palsied children (Hewett 1970), again the majority had taken their child on holiday (71 per cent). Most of them had found accommodation in the usual ways and stayed in hotels, boarding houses, holiday camps or caravans; a few had used special accommodation provided by various bodies interested in the handicapped. However, of those families who had not taken holidays, the reasons were generally unconnected with the handicapped child and were either because they could not afford to or were due to other circumstances like moving house. Only four families had not been able to take a holiday because they could not find suitable accommodation.

Some of the children in this survey had been on special holidays for the handicapped, though many of the mothers thought that this kind of holiday would be more suitable when the child was older, would not mind being away from home and would enjoy the company of other children (the children were aged between one and nine years). Mothers who were not interested in their children going on this type of holiday had only slightly handicapped children, who, from a holiday point of view, were no particular problem, or very handicapped children who were so unaware of their surroundings that there seemed little point in going on such a holiday.

Many handicapped children are now accommodated in hostels or hospitals while their parents take a holiday. The period is usually anything up to eight weeks and gives the parents an opportunity to rest and, if they have non-handicapped children, they can give them full attention and engage in activities which are not possible when the handicapped child is present.

Contact with other children. If the handicapped child is the only child in the family and if he does not attend school or special care unit during the day, he can be very restricted in his contacts with other children, though there are, or course, non-handicapped young children in the same position. Hewett (1970) found that the percentage of handicapped children who were very restricted in their contacts with other children was 13 as compared with 7 per cent of normal four-year-olds.

Attending clinics. It is clear that most handicapped children attend clinics of various kinds far more often than do non-handicapped children. For many families, this is not too much of a problem and is an accepted part of life. Difficulties arise for some families if transport is a problem, if both parents work and need to take time off to attend, or if the child dislikes attending clinics and resists going or is difficult when he is there.

Housing. Some families find that as the handicapped child grows up, their house becomes inadequate and features of it add to the care-problems of the child. In the Isle of Wight survey, twelve of the fifty-nine families with physically disabled children and eighteen of the forty-six with brain dysfunction had had housing problems. Houses with badly planned bathrooms, awkward stairs, difficulty of access to the toilet or narrow doorways can present problems. Sometimes it is necessary to make arrangements for the handicapped child to sleep downstairs to avoid a struggle to get him up the stairs. The location of a house can be difficult too; not having a garden is a disadvantage for any family with children but a greater one if the child is handicapped, needs supervision for longer and is not able to go to a park or playground by himself. Being near to busy roads with fast traffic is difficult too. Some families buy a new house because of the handicapped child; a bungalow is often found to be more convenient.

Costs. It is generally agreed that it costs more to have a handicapped child than a non-handicapped one. Extra costs can arise from needing to change houses or from finding a car essential. Most handicapped children wear out clothes and shoes more quickly and if the child is incontinent, laundry costs and increased wear of bedclothes is added. Sometimes the mother would have ordinarily gone out to work to help the family budget; the presence of a handicapped child makes this much more difficult.

Providing adequate stimulation. Many handicapped children miss experiences which normal children have in the normal course of everyday life. The mentally handicapped are not always taken out as much or involved in activities in the home because they seem to be less able to benefit. The physically handicapped child is often more difficult to take around and is likely to have more absences from home than a non-handicapped child. Cashdan (1968) reports an interesting experiment which illustrates this point with three groups of children who were all of the same mental age. He used three tests to discover how familiar each child was with different

59

kinds of object. The test materials consisted of plastic bags each containing five objects and each bag was designed to test the child's knowledge of a particular situation. The first test covered 'Outings and Occasions': the child had to pick out of one bag the object he would see at the zoo, out of another something that he would see at the swimming baths, and so on. The second test covered everyday-life situations – like a hairdresser's salon, a garage and shops; the third test assessed familiarity with adult activities, using domestic objects. On these tests both the physically handicapped and the mentally handicapped recognized fewer objects than normal four-year-olds who had the same mental age.

He also interviewed mothers to assess the degree of stimulation and the amount of affection given. On his assessment of the amount of stimulation given, the normal children had received most, the mentally handicapped less and the physically handicapped least. On the assessments of affection shown, the physically and mentally handicapped children appeared similar and received less affection than did the normal children. However, those were group differences; and looking at the individual scores, some mothers of mentally handicapped children produced as high scores as did the highest scoring mothers of normal children. The differences occurred in those with lower scores, and there were more very low scores in the mentally handicapped group.

Feelings of inadequacy. Mothers of handicapped children sometimes feel inadequate to cope with the task of rearing the child and become critical of themselves. Hewett (1970) points out, however, that many features traditionally mentioned as characterizing mothers of handicapped children may also be common in mothers of normal children, and she illustrates from a study of mothers of normal four-year-olds in Nottingham. More than half of these mothers were critical of themselves as mothers and they often said that they felt guilty because they failed to be the kind of mother that they felt was ideal.

Rearing a handicapped child does not consist only of problems, however. In the East Midlands sample (Hewett 1970) 90 per cent of the mothers saw their cerebral palsied children as being happy most of the time and 66 per cent of the children were seen as both happy and easy to manage. 69 per cent were felt not to be particularly demanding, though a minority of 31 per cent wanted to follow the mother around or to be with her all the time.

Effects of a handicapped child on parental relationship

On the whole, having a handicapped child does not often affect the relationship of the parents, though if the marriage is unstable it seems that the handicap of the child may add an extra problem.

The Isle of Wight study (Rutter *et al.* 1970) found that the only frequently mentioned problem caused by the child was that of the parents quarrelling about how to look after the child and what he should be allowed to do. A minority of the families had this problem, seventeen of the fifty-nine parents of physically disabled children and twenty of the forty-six who had children with brain dysfunction.

Hewett (1970) found a great deal of agreement amongst the parents. 67 per cent of the mothers of these children said that they and their husbands agreed about the upbringing of their handicapped child. There appeared to be a considerable amount of disharmony in a few families but it did not seem likely that having a handicapped child had any effect on this – these families would probably have been disharmonious without the child. There were thirty-one children from the East Midlands area whose mothers would have been included in this survey had the child not been in residential care. This may have excluded some 'high disagreement' families, if this kind of family is more likely to seek residential care for the child. However, even if all these thirty-one children were counted as being from families where there was parental disagreement, the amount of disagreement in the sample would be no more than was found in the families of normal children.

Studies of parents of children with spina bifida have found that the birth of a handicapped child had an initial uniting effect on the parents but that marital stress was likely to be felt later. Higher divorce and separation rates than normal have been found but it has usually been felt that the child was not the only cause. These marriages were already at risk and the handicapped child produced the extra stress which caused the breakdown. Where families remained united the parents had been married for at least five years and the child had been planned and wanted.

Effects of further children

It has sometimes been found that the birth of a normal child subsequent to having a handicapped one has the effect of reducing stress in the parents. However, a significant number of parents are deterred from having another child by the presence of the handicapped one, either through fear that the next child might be handicapped too or because the handicapped child is so difficult to look after that they could not cope with a baby as well. Thus the decision as to whether to have another child is less of a problem for those with a mildly handicapped child.

In the East Midlands survey of 180 families with children with cerebral palsy (Hewett 1970), about half of the mothers said that their feelings about whether to have another child or not had not changed. Three had had another specifically because of the handicapped one. However, 34 per cent said that they had been deterred from having another child or that they had had another but would have preferred not to.

Effects of a handicapped child on his siblings

It has been suggested that the brothers and sisters of handicapped children can be affected in several ways: they may be neglected in favour of the handicapped child; more pressure may be put on them to be successful to compensate for the handicapped one; as they grow up they may be embarrassed by the handicapped member of the family and be reluctant to take friends home.

When a child is affected by the handicap of his sibling, depth studies have suggested the following basic reactions: that he feels guilt because he pestered his parents for a brother or sister; he feels that the handicapped child is spoiled, gets his own way or has excessive parental attention; he finds it difficult to explain his brother or sister to his friends, feeling that the handicapped condition is a reflection on the family.

However, the majority of siblings of handicapped children are not detectably affected by the presence of the handicapped child in the home. The number of siblings who are affected varies from study to study depending on what criteria are used. One study showed that a quarter of the siblings of children with congenital heart disease had behavioural problems or psychosomatic disorders. Another found that siblings of children with spina bifida were four times as likely to have scores in the maladjusted range on an assessment of social adjustment and eight times as likely to have scores in the unsettled range.

However, the first of two related studies of siblings of children with Down's Syndrome and of children with a cleft palate found no more problems than in a comparison group on non-handicapped children. In the second study, however, elder sisters of mentally handicapped children appeared to be at greater risk of psychiatric disorder.

There is some evidence that siblings' reactions to the handi-capped child are related to their parents' reactions. It has also been suggested that siblings of lightly handicapped children are more often found to be maladjusted than those of the heavily handicapped.

Findings from the Isle of Wight study also suggest that it is only a minority of siblings who are affected. Parents were asked if the presence of the handicapped child deterred the other child from entertaining his friends at home. Five of the fifty-nine families with physically disabled children and nine of the forty-six with a child with brain dysfunction said it did.

Hewett (1970) reports that both mothers of normal four-year-olds and mothers of children with cerebral palsy were asked if other children in the family ever seemed jealous of the four-year-old or the physically handicapped child respectively. In both cases, 33 per cent of the sample reported some jealousy. In this study, many mothers said that they deliberately paid extra attention to the normal children to make up for the extra attention needed by the handicapped one but the majority felt that jealousy was not much of a problem. They sometimes found that on occasions people outside the family tended to favour the handicapped child. The 180 mothers were asked if they were worried about the behaviour of their normal children. Only eleven said they were and in eight of these cases there were other possible causes such as disrupted fathering or marital discord.

Different approaches to discipline could be difficult to explain to the children and both directions of sibling reactions were expressed: in some cases they felt that the handicapped child should never be punished and in other cases they showed resentment if he was not punished. Only a few siblings (13 per cent) tended to resent necessary discriminations, for example that the physically handicapped child had help in dressing.

On the whole, it appeared that siblings' feelings were mixed, rather than being clearly tolerant or clearly resentful.

Methods of helping families

Group discussions and regular meetings for relatives of handicapped people are increasing in popularity. Very few of these have been evaluated in detail and little is known of what happens to attitudes and feelings in the course of these discussions but they are almost always felt to be beneficial. They can be used to provide information, as a forum for problem-solving and mutual assistance; they help participants to feel that they are not alone in coping with their problems and they produce pressure groups to aim at improvements in services and facilities.

In the majority of studies where either the handicapped or their relatives have been asked about information received, it is noticeable that they very frequently say that they have not received enough. This may partly reflect the fact that many of the questions asked are unanswerable at the present time: it is often not possible to say what caused the handicap, or to predict exactly what the child will achieve in the future. It may also be due to the fact that not all information given during one session with a consultant is retained. It is known that patients leaving a doctor's surgery remember only a proportion of what they are told. Parents taking their handicapped child for consultation are usually anxious and often distracted by whether the child is behaving himself and whether he is showing himself at his best. Having regular group meetings can help parents to catch up on information and listen to invited speakers in a more relaxed state.

One dissonant view is that membership of a Parents Society can in some cases increase anxiety and frustration, perhaps because parents become fully aware of every possible problem rather than just their own.

Also being introduced – though they are largely in an experimental stage – are (1) workshops to help parents assess and teach their own child; (2) arrangements for social workers specially trained in the latest methods of developing desired behaviour and reducing behaviour problems to visit parents and children in their homes; and (3) toy libraries to increase the range of play equipment available to the handicapped child.

5
Cognitive, motor and educational deficits

Many handicaps involve problems of cognitive development –
uneven progress in the processes by which we perceive our
surroundings, learn, understand and remember facts about the
world and act appropriately (see C2).

In practice, facts about cognitive or motor deficits are
expressed in several ways, according to the methods used to
discover them.

Methods of assessing cognitive and motor deficits

In some cases an intelligence test is used. This consists of a
standard list of questions to be asked and tasks to be performed
and the subject receives a score on the basis of the number he
gets right or performs successfully. This score is then compared
with the scores of his own age group in the standardization
sample – the large group of people who were tested when the
test was produced to provide norms or standards for the test
scores. If the individual being tested has a score which is
exactly average for his age group, his IQ will be 100 on every
test in common use today. Other scores represent his position
in relation to those of the same age in terms of what proportion
scores higher than he does and what proportion scores lower.
Tests vary as to which IQ scores represent each proportion of
the age group. However, the most usual use of IQ scores, as it
relates to the handicapped, is as follows: the range of normal
intelligence is considered as being from IQ eighty upwards,

and this includes low average, average, high average and superior intelligence as the figures increase. The range from seventy to eighty IQ is a borderline range between subnormality and normality, the mildly mentally handicapped have IQs in the fifty to seventy IQ range and those with an IQ below fifty are normally classified as severely subnormal. This classification system is by no means generally agreed, and opinions and practices vary as to which IQ figures mark the limits for each category. As any person's IQ rating is likely to vary from occasion to occasion and according to which test is being used, it is inadvisable to insist on hard and fast categories when describing the individual. However, for descriptions of groups, this system seems to be the most commonly used.

IQ tests are used to describe the overall intellectual functioning of groups of people and are usually based on assessment of a range of cognitive abilities.

Sometimes a developmental scale of assessment is used to assess whether any particular group has a deficit; for example, if speech is being assessed it is convenient to express results in terms of a language age or speech age. In this situation, the ability of the person being assessed is recorded and compared, not with his own age group, but with what is found to be average for other age groups. So a group of mentally retarded people may be found to have language ages between four years and two years when their actual ages are ten to eleven years; this would mean that from the point of view of their language, they have developed their skills to a level between that of the average four-year-old and that of the average two-year-old.

In some cases of deficit it is more convenient not to use a scale for measurement – as when an intelligence scale or a mental age scale is used – but to classify subjects into two groups, those with adequate ability and those who have a defect. This would occur when speech articulation is categorized as impaired or unimpaired, when distractibility and difficulty in paying attention to what is required is recorded as present or absent, or when aspects of visual perception are considered a problem or not a problem.

A final method of describing deficits which has been used is the experimental method. Here two or more groups of subjects – one of the groups representing a normal, non-handicapped population – are given the same task under exactly the same conditions and their performance is compared to see if one group performs better than another. For example, a group of normal children, a group of mentally retarded children, and a group of autistic children might be given a task of pressing a button every time a green light shows on a control panel, but not when a red one appears. The three groups could then be compared to see if any group has slower reaction times or a greater number of errors.

Methods of assessing educational deficits

Here an age standard is almost always used. Tests of attainment in a particular subject which have been standardized on a large group of children of various ages are given, and attainment on any one aspect of an educational skill is compared with the average attainment of various age groups. Reading tests may include measures of accuracy of reading words, sentences or paragraphs, speed of reading or comprehension of what has been read. Arithmetic tests measure either speed of working or accuracy and may be of mental or written arithmetic. Spelling tests usually measure accuracy. So a particular child might be said to have a reading age of seven years, in that he reads as well as the average seven-year-old, an arithmetic age of six and a half years, and a spelling age of five years.

One problem in using this kind of educational attainment test is to make sure that the standards are currently relevant. After a few years, we cannot be sure that what half of the seven-year-olds in the population could read then is the same as what they can read now. Educational methods and practices, such as the age at which the child is introduced to reading, can influence age standards. For this reason, if the reading ages of a group of handicapped children are being investigated a group of non-handicapped children is often tested at the same time to see if the reading ages of the test are still appropriate or are correct for a particular school or area of residence.

In general there is a relationship between cognitive deficit and educational deficit. In most cases of intellectual retardation, we expect educational retardation too, though on some aspects of attainment the relationship is not particularly strong. Reading accurately, for example, is on the whole affected by lower intelligence, but some people with IQs of perhaps fifty or sixty can read very accurately and others with higher IQs of seventy or eighty are unable to read. Spelling is, in general, poorer in people with lower intelligence but there are variations unrelated to IQ. Arithmetic is much more closely related to intelligence level.

In people of unimpaired intelligence, however, there may still be an educational deficit. In this case we need to look for other relevant factors.

Factors influencing cognitive deficit

The main differentiating factor between handicapped people who have cognitive deficits and those who do not, appears to be whether the brain is involved in the handicap. In the Isle of Wight study (Rutter *et al.* 1970) the performance on an intelligence test of children with physical handicaps which involved the brain was compared with the performance of children with physical disorders which did not involve the brain, such as asthma, eczema, deafness, orthopaedic disorders, heart disease, diabetes, paralysis following poliomyelitis and muscular dystrophy. The intelligence test performance of this latter group was very similar to the performance of a group of non-handicapped children used for comparison. The group of children whose handicap involved the brain, and who had either uncomplicated epilepsy or evidence of structural brain damage, including Down's Syndrome, had markedly lower scores. Fourteen of the children were too retarded to score on the test used and had a severe mental handicap. However, there were differences within this group as the children with uncomplicated epilepsy did not score lower than non-handicapped children; the deficits were found only in the performance of children with structural brain damage.

Apart from deficits arising directly from the condition, another kind of influence has been considered to be lack of experience either from the limitations of the handicap itself or from the background in which the person lives. Many handicapped children develop more slowly than normal, because their experiences are more restricted, even though they may reach an eventual normal level. Motor handicap, blindness and deafness have all been found to have a developmentally retarding effect at some stage. Additionally, there is evidence that an unstimulating cultural background can affect any child's development and that intellectual attainment is likely to be affected by little conversation or restricted interests in the home, poor attendance at school and a general lack of interest in intellectual pursuits in the family. A handicapped child is likely to be affected by his background to the same extent as a normal one, if not more so.

Factors influencing educational attainment

The two factors mentioned above as influencing cognitive development have also been considered as affecting educational attainment. Progress in education may be impeded by factors arising directly from the handicap, such as difficulties of learning, attending and concentrating or difficulties in visual and auditory perception; lack of experience has again been thought to be an influence in retarding educational attainments either because the handicap itself prevents the child from experiencing many of the things he has to learn about or because his home does not give him as much educational experience as most.

Various other factors have also been suggested as relevant in considering what makes a handicapped child more likely to be educationally retarded.

Absences from school are more common for many handicapped children. On his return from a period of absence, the child will have missed out on new information that his classmates have learned; if they have been taught an important aspect of a particular subject – like a reading rule or a process in arithmetic – he may well find that he does not understand what everyone else is doing. Unless the teacher has time to give him extra tuition, which is not always possible in a large class, he is likely to become confused, frustrated or depressed and be less likely to try to do well. It has been suggested that a single period of absence is not too damaging but that a series of absences have a marked detrimental effect. The increased absences from school of many handicapped children are generally due to increasing needs to go into hospital or attend clinics, periods of illness due directly to the handicap or due to a side-effect – such as respiratory diseases in physically disabled and mentally retarded children, or problems of transport if special transport arrangements are needed. Problems of being absent from school to go into hospital are ameliorated to some extent by the provisions of classes in hospital wards.

It has been felt too that where drugs are used in treatment of the handicap, these may have a retarding effect. This problem arises mainly in cases of epilepsy, when it is occasionally difficult to find a level where the child's fits are controlled and he does not become too drowsy. Attempts to demonstrate the effects of anti-convulsant drugs have not produced any clear results, however, and this may not be an important factor.

It has been suggested that another factor contributing to educational retardation is lowered expectations of parents and teachers regarding the handicapped child's performance. Because allowances are made for the child's disability, pressures to do well are avoided and signs of falling behind in school work are attributed to his disability rather than seen as something which should be remedied.

Whatever the factors involved, it is clear that physical disability, whether the brain is affected or not, is related to lowered educational attainment. The Isle of Wight survey (Rutter *et al.* 1970) found that all the groups of children with a physical disorder where the brain is not involved, contained children who had problems in reading. On the whole they had reading accuracy levels of nine months below their actual age and reading comprehension levels six months below. All the groups of children with physical disorder contained children who were at least twenty-four months behind in reading. When the effect of intelligence was allowed for, and the reading level that would be expected on the basis of the children's actual age and measured IQ was calculated, 14 per cent of the children with physical disorder were shown to be reading at a level at least twenty-eight months behind what would be expected, whereas in the non-handicapped the rate was just under five and a half per cent. The group of children who had physical disorder where the brain was involved was more retarded in reading; on average, they were two years behind the average attainment of their age group in both reading accuracy and reading comprehension. This retardation could not be entirely explained by lowered intelligence as when IQ was allowed for, over a quarter of the children were retarded in reading by at least twenty-eight months which was considerably greater than the frequency of five and a half per cent found in the non-handicapped children. School absences may have been relevant but did not entirely explain the results of the survey. The researchers found that children with brain disorder were absent more often from school than non-handicapped children. However, children with uncomplicated epilepsy were not absent much more often than average, and yet they had some reading retardation; moreover, the school absence rate was the same for children whose physical disorders did not involve the brain as for children whose handicaps did involve the brain, but the reading retardation was much greater in the latter group. So school absences were a possible contributing factor but did not fully account for the rates of retardation. It was concluded that the reading retardation of the brain disorder group was partly due, also, to the direct effects of brain dysfunction.

We shall now consider some of the findings in relation to specific groups of handicapped children which relate to cognitive or educational deficit.

Autism

Whether autistic children have been found to have lowered intelligence levels or not, and how frequent this finding is, depends to some extent on which children have been included in the diagnostic group of autism. Some writers have excluded mentally handicapped children with features of autism, others include them. What is certainly clear is that when intelligence levels of autistic children are measured by intelligence tests, the results range from findings of normal intelligence in some cases to severe mental handicap in others, and that there is a bias towards the lower levels of intelligence. One study (Lotter, 1966) of thirty-two children diagnosed as autistic found that twenty-two of the children had IQs below fifty-five and six had IQs below eighty. Only the remaining four had intelligence levels in the normal range, three being of average intelligence and one above average.

Rutter *et al.* (1967) assessed sixty-three children who had attended the Maudsley Hospital Children's Department from 1950 to 1958 and for whom a diagnosis of 'child psychosis, schizophrenic syndrome of childhood, infantile autism or any synonyms of these' had been agreed by the psychiatrists who saw the child. Of these sixty-three children, ten were unable to score or to co-operate well enough to score on any of the tests used and there was no evidence that their IQs were above fifty. Of the fifty-three who were tested, seventeen had IQs of fifty or below, eighteen had IQs between fifty-one and seventy, twelve had IQs between seventy-one and ninety and six had IQs of ninety-one to a hundred and twenty. Although autistic children can be very difficult to test, and in this study the psychologist often felt that the result was not a particularly valid measure of the child's intelligence, the scores proved to be very stable and

71

were remarkably similar when the children were reassessed between five and fifteen years later.

These children were compared with another group of children who had the same range of intelligence levels and who had various diagnoses but were not autistic, and several other deficits in the autistic children are apparent. Speech was retarded in all the sixty-three autistic children, either because it had never developed, or it had developed and been lost again; delayed speech was found in fifty-three of the sixty-three non-autistic children and so was common in this group too but not as universal. Later, the autistic children were found more likely to have a short attention-span or poor persistence – thirty-five of them showed this characteristic as opposed to seventeen of the non-autistic group. They were, however, less likely to be distractible; only two of the autistic children were, as compared with twelve of the non-autistic group.

Within the overall intelligence test scores there was evidence of variability in the levels the autistic children achieved; they tended to find verbal tasks more difficult, and found it harder to deal with tasks involving abstract thought or symbolism or sequential logic. They were at their best on tasks that required manipulative or visuo-spatial skills or tests requiring immediate recall of verbal material. These differences appeared to be due to defects in the use and understanding of language and are consistent with the finding that they all had delayed language development.

That an intellectual deficit is extremely common in autism seems clear, but what the actual nature of the deficit is is still being debated. One theory is that although the autistic child's eyes and ears function normally, he cannot make sense of the incoming information and particularly cannot co-ordinate information from each of the senses to form a meaningful whole. Another theory is that autistic children have never learned that objects are permanent and so cannot develop language, as it is difficult to learn to name an object when it is not understood as having a permanent independent existence. A third theory suggests that stimuli are too intense for the autistic child and his odd behaviour is a defence against being over-aroused. These and several more theories are currently being investigated, and most investigators feel that whatever the nature of the deficit, it is probably due to delayed development in some parts of the brain, and that the major symptom lies in abnormality of response to environmental stimuli.

Blindness

As blindness does not necessarily involve the brain, no cognitive deficit is expected to occur apart from those involved in lack of sight. There is some evidence that young blind children develop more slowly through the early stages of co-ordinating their unimpaired senses and their movements but eventually other senses are developed to compensate for poor sight. Only when blindness is part of a multiply-handicapped condition, which includes brain damage, are there likely to be marked cognitive deficits.

It has been thought that abstract concepts may be more difficult to learn if evidence from one of the senses is missing. One experiment showed, however, that concepts like 'pride', 'fear', 'sadness' can be appreciated tactually by older school children. The experiment (Dershowitz 1973) was conducted with boys and girls aged eight to sixteen, some of whom were blind and some sighted. Flat designs cut out of asbestos tile and standing clay forms were designed to represent the various concepts. Each one was presented to the subject, who was asked which of two concepts it represented for him, for instance whether it represented anger or peace. The sighted children were blindfolded for one test and also given the test as a visual appreciation exercise. Results showed that blind children could appreciate these concepts tactually as well as could sighted children who were blindfolded, but did not perform better; the sighted children's visual perception of these properties was superior to the blind children's tactile perception of them.

Brain disorder

We saw earlier in the chapter that handicapped children whose brain is involved in their handicap are more likely to have both educational and intellectual deficits.

When the brain is involved in the handicap, it is likely too that there will be some difficulties of visual perception, by which we mean that the eyes are seeing correctly but the brain is not able to make the normal contribution of organizing the information the eyes take in. Many people with cerebral palsy or with brain dysfunction have these difficulties, which are often hard to detect but which can have a profound effect. For example, the affected person may have difficulty in paying attention to the desired object if there are too many visual distractions: he may, for example, have difficulty in picking up a knife and fork from a laden dinner table or finding a book on a crowded desk. It has been pointed out that this is not a state which we commonly call 'not paying attention' but is due to attending to too many things at the same time or attending to the wrong ones. Sometimes a child will have difficulty in recognizing horizontal and vertical lines, which makes moving around, particularly through doorways, a problem. Again, the affected person may fail to notice something relevant through a failure in the visual scanning of his surroundings and accidents may occur when he falls over or bumps into something he did not see. Visual perception problems are probably related to the clumsiness often seen to accompany brain damage.

Difficulty in discriminating between right and left has also been found more common in brain-damaged children.

In most cases of perceptual deficit, the condition is generally felt to be directly due to incomplete or delayed maturity of parts of the brain where the damage has occurred.

The attention deficit in brain damage has been experimentally investigated. One experiment (Gorton 1972) compared groups of normal children, mentally retarded children who were diagnosed as brain damaged on the basis of a neurological examination, and mentally retarded children whose retardation was thought to be due to cultural or familial factors. All the children performed arithmetic problems in different surroundings. They all worked better in a cubicle alone than alongside others in an ordinary classroom situation. The normal and the cultural-familial mentally retarded children worked best when they were visually secluded in a cubicle, though whether the cubicle was soundproof or not had no effect on their performance. The brain-damaged mentally retarded group, however, worked best when they were completely secluded from both visual and auditory distractions, working in a soundproof cubicle.

Cerebral palsy

It is usually estimated that about half of the people who have cerebral palsy are mentally handicapped, that a quarter have intelligence levels within the dull-normal range and that a quarter are of average or above average intelligence.

On the whole it has been found that their rate of development is considerably slower than that of physically normal children and that as a group they are particularly slow in learning to speak.

Even when intelligence is normal and the physical disability is mild, there is evidence that a considerable number of people with cerebral palsy have perceptuo-motor difficulties; they may have problems in analysing spatial relationships, in performing simple constructional tasks, in differentiating between left and right and generally in appreciating size, shape and distance. It has been suggested that these frequent perceptual difficulties are partly due directly to damage to the brain but also to limited early experience in activities which help the child to learn to co-ordinate his senses and his limb movements. This latter theory is supported by the findings that perceptual defects sometimes improve with age.

The development and performance of the cerebral palsied is also affected by an increased frequency of sensory defects; for example, one survey found that over 50 per cent of hemiplegic children, whose spasticity affects mainly one side of their body, had sensory defects. Because of the abnormal physical movements involved, sensory defects are often difficult to detect. Hearing losses seem to be particularly common. One investigation (Dunsdon 1952) of twenty-seven people with cerebral palsy who had delayed speech showed that when their hearing was properly investigated only one had completely normal hearing and one had complete hearing on one side and a slight loss on the other. The rest had hearing problems which probably contributed to their lack of speech.

Deafness

When deafness is the only handicap, and the brain is not involved, there is no evidence that intelligence is impaired. As with blindness, cognitive development tends to be a little slower in deaf children when they are compared with non-handicapped children of the same age, but the differences are very small. Although it is often said that those with impaired hearing are particularly visually alert, there is some evidence that in childhood development of visual perception can be slower than in hearing children; one study (Colin and Vurpillot 1971–72) of sixty deaf boys, aged four to seven years old, used a hidden figures task, where the boys had to find figures concealed within a large picture. When compared with hearing boys of the same age, the deaf children gave poorer responses and the strategy they used to make the search was less efficient.

It has been said that deafness is the greatest educational barrier as discussion of abstract material is difficult without speech and easy verbal communication. Some hearing impairment has frequently been found amongst groups of educationally retarded children and undiagnosed and uncorrected hearing loss is certainly a contributory cause in educational backwardness.

Epilepsy

It is generally agreed that epilepsy in itself does not relate to reduced intelligence and that most children who have epilepsy are of normal intelligence. A study of thirteen pairs of monozygotic (identical) twins who were chosen because one of the pair had seizures and one did not, showed that there were no significant differences between their intelligence levels; the average IQ of the twins who had fits was 100·7 and that of the twins without fits was 103·2. In psychometric terms a difference of this size is considered as being so small that it is probably due to chance factors, just as likely to be in the reverse direction if the testing were repeated, and so is considered insignificant. A lower than average intelligence level in an epileptic child is most likely to be found in a child who has a significant amount of brain damage, and where the epilepsy is symptomatic of this.

Educational attainments are more likely to be affected. In the survey of all nine- to eleven-year-olds in the Isle of Wight (Rutter *et al.* 1970), there were fifty-nine children with epilepsy uncomplicated by other conditions or signs of brain damage. The finding of other studies that this group was of average intelligence was confirmed, and their average IQ was found to be 102, but their reading was on average twelve months behind their actual age. Eighteen per cent of the epileptic children were retarded in reading by two years or more, whereas only just under seven per cent of the children with no physical or psychiatric problems, who were used for comparison, were as retarded as this. The investigators felt that the reading retardation was related to brain dysfunction rather than to other possible factors.

Other sources have suggested that arithmetic and spelling may be even more retarded in epileptic children.

The mentally handicapped have more deficits than any other group, and as a general principle, as intellectual level decreases the number of additional handicaps tends to increase.

Most cognitive abilities are impaired in the mentally handicapped. They perform most kinds of learning more slowly, although there is some evidence that on one task of non-verbal rote learning they perform as well as normal people of the same age (the task was learning to associate together in pairs pictures of familiar objects; the subjects were only mildly mentally handicapped). Problem-solving is impaired and constructional ability is poorer on average. The Isle of Wight survey found that in children with IQs below seventy, constructional ability, as assessed by copying shapes with matches, was poor in 34 per cent as compared with just over two per cent of the non-handicapped.

Lack of motor control is more common in the mentally handicapped and poor co-ordination is more often found. 43·4 per cent of children with IQs below seventy in the Isle of Wight survey had poor performance on the Oseretsky Test of Motor Proficiency as compared with five per cent of the normal children. On the positive side, it is thought that on some motor tasks, although their initial performance is poor, the mentally handicapped, given adequate training, can reach levels approaching normal. Motor impersistence – the inability to sustain a voluntary motor act that has been initiated by verbal command like keeping the eyes closed, protruding the tongue or keeping the mouth open, is more marked in the mentally handicapped; 40 per cent of the Isle of Wight sample of retarded children showed marked motor impersistence as compared with five per cent of the normal group. Again on the positive side, the mentally handicapped are said to have good retention of some performance skills and remember tasks that they have been taught well for a very long time.

Sensory defects complicate performance on many tasks and they are more frequently found in the mentally handicapped. One survey of a group of ten- to nineteen-year-olds – who had mental ages of five years and above – in a hospital for the mentally handicapped, found that only 44 per cent of the group had no hearing loss.

Finally, speech and verbal development is slower in the mentally handicapped. It has usually been found that their speech development follows a normal developmental sequence but much more slowly and with a lower than average final level.

In the Isle of Wight study, within the group of children with IQs below seventy a quarter had not used single words until after they were two years old and a quarter did not use three word phrases until after three years. Speech defects are common in the mentally handicapped; estimates of their frequency range from 50 to 82 per cent. In the above study, around half of the children had articulation defects, po⁓r complexity of language and inadequacy of descriptive ability.

It should be appreciated that within the group which is generally termed mentally handicapped there is a wide range of levels from those who are totally disabled by mental, physical and perhaps sensory handicaps, with in some cases epilepsy too, to those who may have IQs around seventy but who are not too obviously different from the normal population. The frequency and extent of deficits will vary accordingly.

Muscular dystrophy

For many years there has been a controversy as to whether people with muscular dystrophy are more likely to be mentally retarded. A lower average IQ in groups of subjects with Duchenne-type progressive muscular dystrophy has often been found, but there has been argument as to whether lowered intelligence is directly related to the disease or whether it is due to deprivation of experience by physical limitations. The situation seems to be that the intelligence levels of people with progressive muscular dystrophy cover the same range as normal but the average is typically eighty IQ rather than a hundred and there is an increased incidence of mental retardation; one study (Cohen et al. 1968) of 211 patients with progressive muscular dystrophy found that 21 per cent were mentally retarded, but there was no increased rate of mental retardation amongst their siblings who were not dystrophic. As Duchenne-type dystrophy is genetically caused, there is sometimes more than one affected boy in a family; when brothers with dystrophy are compared their intelligence levels are very similar. Where there is mental retardation, it is usually felt to be due to organic impairment to the brain, but no clear structural or chemical abnormalities have been found.

Spina bifida

Intelligence in children with spina bifida has been found to vary with the type of lesion, the sex of the child and with the presence or absence and severity of hydrocephalus.

In children with spina bifida without hydrocephalus, IQ is normally distributed. Hydrocephalus, if present and extensive, is likely to cause lowered intelligence, motor inco-ordination and defective visual perception. Females have been found to be more likely to be intellectually impaired than males (it has been speculated that severely affected boys are less likely to survive).

Children with spina bifida are often educationally backward. One study found an average reading retardation of eighteen months and of thirty months in arithmetic ages. Spelling is also retarded on average. One likely cause is that these children have frequent periods of hospitalization and sometimes enter school late. It has been estimated that three-quarters of them are in need of skilled remedial help in educational skills.

Conclusion

A general conclusion is that when the brain is involved in a handicap, cognitive abilities are likely to be impaired and that a child with any form of handicap is at risk of being educationally retarded to a greater or lesser extent. Within any group of children, however, attainments also depend on such factors as motivation, interest and the minimizing of frustration.

6
Personality and behaviour disturbance

The structure of personality and the incidence and type of behaviour disturbances in the handicapped are difficult to study as different researchers have used varying definitions, methods and personality theories on which to base their work (see D1 and D3). Conclusions are reached in terms of personality structure, personality disorder, emotional disturbance, behavioural disturbance or disorder and mental illness, and these concepts often overlap.

The fundamental questions to be asked, however, would seem to be whether the handicapped have identifiably different personalities from the non-handicapped and whether they are more prone to behaviour which is unacceptable to themselves or to others.

Methods of study

Most writers feel that special methods and separate personality theories are not needed when studying the handicapped but that they can usually be assessed using the same theories of structure and by the same methods as with the non-handicapped. Many methods of assessing personality are, however, based on verbal reports and responses to questions about how a particular person feels and behaves, and his attitudes towards others. This raises a particular problem when verbal communication with a handicapped person is limited.

Exceptions to the general rule that special theories have not been felt necessary are some studies of personality among the mentally handicapped. Here some special theories have been introduced, for example, the rigidity explanation of the behaviour of retarded people, which suggests that the mentally handicapped tend to repeat the same behaviour patterns, are less likely to try new ones, and are less inclined to transfer a response made in one situation into another. The social learning theory approach assesses the handicapped person in terms of the individual's preference for any particular reinforcement (reward) and his expectation that it will occur as the result of his behaviour.

In the handicap field in general, four basic methods have been used:

Questionnaire to subject. The same questionnaires or other verbal methods that are used in the general population have been applied, and in some cases attempts have been made to simplify the questionnaires used so that they can be understood and completed by the less intelligent person, whose reading is more limited.

Questionnaire about the subject. In this case a questionnaire is given to the parents of the person being assessed or to someone who knows him well. It may be in the form of a specified list of questions or an interview where the interviewer has specific questions to answer, but the person being interviewed is encouraged to talk freely and the interviewer decides on the eventual answer.

Direct observation of behaviour. When communication with the subject is limited, it is often best to observe him to see how he behaves and make an assessment of his personality or problems on the basis of these observations.

Experimental observations of behaviour. Groups of subjects may be observed performing the same task under the same conditions and comparisons made between them to assess their type of reaction.

Personality

Most studies have focussed on personality disturbances but a few are aimed at investigating personality structure or type, usually when these are felt to be significantly different from normal.

One study (Wilcox and Smith 1973) used a personality questionnaire to study a group of 101 mildly mentally handicapped children. Retarded boys differed on nearly every one of the fourteen factors from the normal boys; they appeared to be 'less co-operative, much less intelligent, less stable, more demanding, less cheerful, less persevering, much more tough minded, more individualistic, more shrewd, more depressed, less self-controlled, and more tense'. The only scales that did not produce differences were those assessing assertive-rebellious and adventurous-friendly characteristics. Retarded girls showed considerable differences too; they were 'much less co-operative, far less intelligent, less stable, more demanding, more assertive, somewhat less cheerful, less persevering, less friendly, much more individualistic and realistic, more depressed, somewhat less self-controlled and more tense than normal girls'. It was felt that differences in intelligence level or in the way that the retarded children answered the questions may have affected the results and there was an additional complication, in that there were more children from broken homes within the retarded group. Girls seemed particularly affected by this factor and it seemed that apparent personality differences could have been related to familial instability rather than to the mental handicap alone.

Again working with the mentally handicapped, Cromwell (1963) uses the social learning theory approach mentioned above. He predicts that retarded persons will have less expectation of success than normal, and will tend towards avoiding failure rather than seeking success. This tendency is felt to have arisen because retarded people will have had fewer successes in the past. This tendency can be demonstrated experimentally. A typical task is to give the subject two puzzles to complete; he is allowed to finish one but not the other. Later he is given a choice of repeating the one on which he succeeded or attempting again the one on which he failed. His choice indicates whether he is aiming at success, by attempting the uncompleted one, or avoiding failure by repeating the one he has already demonstrated he can do.

A third example of personality description of the handicapped was concerned with deaf clients who were being rehabilitated (Bolton 1972). Their rehabilitation counsellors were given forty-two adjectives and were asked to indicate which were most descriptive and which least descriptive of each client. Four types of personality emerged. Almost one half of the clients were described as 'cheerful, energetic and co-operative'; a second type was described as 'passive, shy, reserved, pleasant, and withdrawn'; the third type was 'defensive, suspicious, stubborn, impulsive'; and the fourth type was 'nervous, cautious, worried and teachable'. These four types corresponded well with the typologies suggested by others.

Behaviour disturbance

Much more attention has been paid to the frequency and type of behaviour disturbance in the handicapped. Though concepts like maladjustment and emotional disturbance may not refer to exactly the same types of behaviour, we shall consider some of the findings in all these areas as they have been related to different handicaps.

Cerebral palsy

It is generally agreed that the incidence of behaviour disturbance is greater in cerebral palsy than in the non-handicapped but estimates of how much greater vary. At the extreme, it has been suggested that one half of those who have cerebral palsy with fits have a psychiatric disorder as do a third of those without fits. However, a survey of fifty-four spastic school leavers found that six people (about 11 per cent) had shown definite signs of psychological disturbance in that they had received or been offered psychiatric treatment. The differences in these two estimates may be due to different definitions of disturbance or perhaps to treatment having been offered, in the second case, to fewer children than needed it.

Particular problems which face the cerebral palsied adolescent have often been mentioned, and there is a suggestion that adolescence is a particularly difficult time for the handicapped. At this stage, they become more aware of peer reaction, of activities they cannot take part in like dancing or athletics, of feelings of being unattractive, of the realities of the work situation, and in some cases they need to give up a fantasy that they will be cured by the time they are grown up. All of these factors have been thought to contribute to psychiatric disturbance in the cerebral palsied adolescent.

There appears to be an increased frequency of temper tantrums in cerebral palsied children. In Hewett's (1970) survey of mothers of 180 cerebral palsied children in the East Midlands, the number of children who never had temper tantrums was the same as for normal four-year-olds, 32 per cent of the latter never had temper tantrums and 31 per cent of the cerebral palsy children never did. However, the frequencies of tantrums varied and daily or almost-daily occurrence was reported more than twice as often in the cerebral palsy group where the proportions were 22 per cent in comparison to 9 per cent in the normal. It seemed that a high proportion of children who had frequent tantrums had lack of speech or severe communication difficulties and could not express their feelings verbally or make requests; frustration may have played a part in these outbursts. Certainly daily or almost-daily temper tantrums were three times as common in children with both mental and physical handicaps as they were in physically handicapped children of normal intelligence; the degree of physical handicap was not related to the frequency of temper tantrums. It was recognized, however, that what mothers of handicapped children called a temper tantrum was not necessarily as clearly defined as for mothers of normal children and to call various behaviours temper tantrums is more of an interpretation when dealing with the severely handicapped.

Temper tantrums have been mentioned as frequent, however, in older people with cerebral palsy and one study of school leavers indicates that 42 per cent of the mildly handicapped with cerebral palsy were known to have temper tantrums which seemed to be beyond their control.

Epilepsy
There is little evidence of a personality pattern common to all people with epilepsy. However, most researchers agree that there is an increased incidence of neurotic problems and character disturbances amongst epileptic people and these are generally thought to be due to surrounding factors such as anxiety about having a·fit, about the social consequences and about whether to reveal the problem.

The main types of disorder found are generally agreed amongst studies, though when the disorders are analysed in more detail, there are many contradictions between conclusions.

Bagley (1971) summarizes the main types of disorder as follows:

1 a neurotic picture with anxiety, depression, fears and inhibition;
2 aggression with temper tantrums and antisocial behaviour;
3 overactive and hyperkinetic behaviour;
4 mental defect.

An interaction theory to account for behaviour disturbances has been suggested where the pre-fit personality, the onset of fits, the reaction of the environment to the fits and the child's reaction to all these, interact with each other in producing eventual behaviour.

Bagley studied 118 children with epilepsy and found that their behaviour could be divided into two clear categories, aggressive and anxious, and that these categories were similar to those found in studies of non-epileptic children. He used independent ratings by two workers on thirty-nine items of possible disturbed behaviour. On the basis of these ratings the 118 children could be divided into four categories, containing fairly similar numbers. 22 per cent scored above the halfway point on both aggressive and anxious behaviour, 25 per cent on aggressive behaviour only, 24 per cent on anxious behaviour only, and 29 per cent were below the midway scores on both.

He also estimated that 43 per cent of the 118 had psychiatric disturbances as great as those which would be seen in a child guidance clinic and amongst the 118 were ten children who seemed to be more disturbed than practically all non-epileptic child guidance clinic children.

Behaviour disorders were related to adverse factors in the child's environment. Conditions like overcrowding, poverty, death or desertion of a parent, clearly distinguished between epileptic children with or without behaviour disorder of all kinds – anxious, aggressive or both. It appeared that there were significantly more adverse factors in the environment in those cases where a near relative also had epilepsy.

It has often been suggested that strong emotion can trigger fits; fright, anxiety, excitement, fear, guilt, frustration have all been considered as likely to produce an attack in an epileptic person.

Mental handicap
Increased likelihood of behaviour disturbance has almost universally been found. One study of mildly mentally handicapped children suggested that there were three times as many

85

who were maladjusted as there were amongst children of normal intelligence. Features of the maladjusted behaviour were depression, inhibition, tension and aggression towards adults, and maladjustment appeared commoner in the older children than the younger ones. Again, other factors besides the handicap were relevant. Those who were maladjusted more often had unstable family backgrounds, were more often in poor health, and had more physical defects.

Various reasons have been suggested for the increased incidence of behaviour disturbance in the mentally handicapped. As they have more deficiencies, they may feel more frustrations and conflicts, be subjected to more pressures and are more likely to be rejected, overprotected or isolated.

Next to mental handicap itself, behaviour disturbance is the most likely reason for admission to an institution to be requested.

Estimates of the actual frequency of behaviour disturbances in the mentally handicapped vary a great deal according to the definition of disorder used. For example one estimate is that half of the mentally handicapped have serious psychiatric disorder, another that 33 per cent have personality disorders and 7 per cent are mentally ill. It has often been suggested that the type of behaviour disturbance found varies with intellectual level and the higher IQ group is prone to neurotic or antisocial behaviour whilst the lower IQ group is likely to be hyperkinetic or psychotic. (See F3.)

Mental illness has been found in around 10 per cent of the mentally handicapped in several studies and they tend to agree that schizophrenia is the most common form, whereas true depression is rare.

Sensory handicaps

We have grouped together the hearing-impaired and visually-impaired in this context as comparisons have sometimes been made between the effects of these two sensory losses on behaviour.

The basic problem in assessing behaviour disturbance in either case has been the lack of a standard; should the behaviour of people with sensory losses be compared with that of the non-handicapped in attempting to reach an assessment of behaviour disturbance or is it possible to allow for the special problems of sensory loss. If the latter course is taken, much apparently unusual behaviour can be seen as normal or expected in a majority of the deaf or blind.

In childhood, the deaf are often noted to be emotionally withdrawn and to show frequent compulsive traits or rituals that are performed over and over again. These features increase the likelihood that a deaf child may be mistakenly considered to be mentally handicapped or autistic. If the hearing loss can be corrected to any extent, by providing a hearing aid, the child's behaviour is often seen to change dramatically. If his hearing loss were taken into account before the introduction of the hearing aid, he could be seen as adapting quite normally to the stimuli available to him and to be adjusted to his own range of experiences.

Characteristics of older deaf people are said to be self-centredness, rigidity of behaviour, impulsiveness with no anxiety or guilt about their actions, lack of empathy with other people, and poor realization of the effects of their behaviour on other people. Again, these behaviour characteristics can be seen as different from those of the non-handicapped but understandable and predictable in a person whose communication with other people is limited. For example, apparently withdrawn behaviour has been seen as characteristic of some deaf people but in fact, when they appear not to be attending to what is happening in their immediate surroundings, they may be concentrating on what is happening in the background, which hearing people learn about through sounds.

It has been suggested that the deaf are constantly in a state of doubt and need to check frequently whether what they understand to be happening is the same as is understood by others. This may be related to the often-noted suspiciousness of the deaf person. It has been suggested that deaf people are inclined to attempt to rely on their own perceptions and judgements and are rarely over-dependent, whereas the blind tend to rely on the information from others to confirm their observations.

Forms of mental illness have been thought to vary between the blind and the deaf. If depression occurs in a deaf person, it is said to be more likely to take an agitated form with a tendency to suspicion and rarely to be of the retarded form with features of guilt and self-blame. There is no evidence that schizophrenia is more common than in the general population. In the case of neurosis, the type most frequently found in the deaf is said to be the obsessional, compulsive kind whereas the blind tend to the dramatic-histrionic, hysterical kind of disorder. One study of blind people found an increased incidence of neurosis, as measured by responses to a questionnaire. 31 per cent of the blind subjects, as compared with 16 per cent of the sighted subjects who worked in the same organizations, had scores within the neurotic range. More females than males had scores suggesting neurosis and neurosis scores were higher for older people.

Problems of evaluation

A general impression of the literature is that the percentage of behaviour disturbance will be greater among the handicapped than among the general population. However, many studies are difficult to evaluate.

There is probably more variation in terminology in this area than in any other area in the study of handicap. Mental illness, psychiatric disorder, behaviour disturbance, maladjustment, emotional disturbance are just a few of the terms applied. Moreover, as we saw in the case of sensory disturbance, judgements may be made using different standards, and some apparently disordered behaviour may also be seen as adaptive within the person's limits.

A second problem is that we do not always have standards by which to compare findings. The more satisfactory studies assess a non-handicapped group who live, attend school or work in the same surroundings or surroundings as comparable as possible to those of the handicapped group being discussed. In other cases statements are made about the frequency of a particular behaviour in a group but we do not know if the presence of the handicap is relevant as there are no comparable findings for non-handicapped groups.

Difficulties sometimes arise in cases where conclusions have been drawn from selected groups, particularly those who are in residential care. Data on mentally handicapped people who are living in a hospital, for example, is likely to give a different impression from data from a mentally handicapped group living at home, as the former group may be different in ways which are related to its being in hospital. We would expect a hospital group to be more difficult to look after, or less independent, because these are the kinds of reasons which lead to a request for admission.

Finally, there is the problem of extricating the relevant factors. Marked behaviour differences between two groups, one handicapped and one not, may suggest that the handicap produces the behaviour difference. However, when other factors are considered they sometimes emerge as being of greater importance. If adverse factors like poor housing, broken families, disrupted family relationships are more common in the handicapped group, they may be far more relevant to the child's behaviour than the handicap itself.

We know, for example, that sometimes parental attitude is related to the child's behaviour, though it is not always clear whether difficult behaviour in the child causes a more negative parental attitude or is an effect of it. Parental attitudes have mostly been studied either by giving the parents a questionnaire or by interviewing them and making ratings on the basis of interview material.

One survey showed that the more difficult the child's behaviour was in school, the more hostile the parent was towards the school (in this case the children were mildly mentally handicapped). It is not difficult to conclude that this kind of relationship of attitude and behaviour can be interpreted in both directions. A parent whose child's behaviour is difficult may be inclined to blame the school and a child who knows his parents are hostile to the school might be expected not to behave well there. An interaction between the two is the most likely explanation.

Bagley (1971) found that adverse attitudes in parents of epileptic children were commonest in those parents whose children were aggressive. Attitudes of parents with children who were both anxious and aggressive were a little less adverse; next in order were parents with anxious children and these attitudes were only a little different in direction from the attitudes of those parents whose children were neither anxious nor aggressive. Adverse attitudes were related to maternal anxiety, maternal inability to cope with problems, father being critical of the child, and parents taking a non-supportive attitude to problems caused by the child's illness. However, the children's behaviour was also related to a number of environmental problems like poverty, overcrowding, disturbing relatives or substantial change in their environment, such as the death or desertion of a parent or moving house. So there were a variety of interrelated factors, all of which influenced the child's behaviour and affected each other, as parents who had a large number of environmental problems to contend with were more likely to have disturbed attitudes and behaviour too.

It has been pointed out that although schools for maladjusted children are usually provided with the services of a psychiatrist, an educational psychologist and a social worker (see C4) and often have close links with a child guidance clinic, special schools for the handicapped have far fewer provisions although estimates show that the incidence of behaviour problems is comparatively high. Much of the published work on treatment methods is concerned with the mentally handicapped, especially in residential institutions like schools or hospitals.

Psychotherapy

This term is used to cover a wide variety of techniques but basically refers to a situation where a professional worker talks to another person in an attempt to improve that person's psychological condition. Most of the published reports claim some success though it is not likely that failures would be reported. Many studies are difficult to evaluate, however.

The reported effects of psychotherapy sometimes tend to be in rather vague terms and based on judgements rather than on any attempt to measure change. However, where beneficial changes occur in a person who has received psychotherapy, they tend to be changes in emotional state. A few claims of increased IQ following psychotherapy have been made, but are comparatively rare.

Most courses of psychotherapy reported have involved one or two sessions a week, the sessions lasting for an hour or an hour and a half. In many cases, little mention has been made of how the person being treated spent the rest of his time, though there may have been therapeutic influences in other situations. One study (O'Connor and Yonge 1955) which did overcome some of these problems used three groups of subjects, one of which received two psychotherapy sessions a week, another group worked in the same workshop as the first group but did not receive psychotherapy, and the third group received no treatment and did general work around the institution. It was then possible to show that changes which occurred in the psychotherapy group did not occur in the other two groups. Changes that occurred included more positive co-operative participation in group discussions, and positive changes in workshop behaviour and performance.

It has been suggested that directive psychotherapy – where

the therapist directs the conversation and initiates and reacts in discussion – is most effective with the more antisocial, aggressive or delinquent mentally handicapped person, whereas non-directive therapy – where the therapist plays a passive role – is more suitable for the withdrawn, shy or anxious person.

If verbal communication with the handicapped person is not possible, play therapy may be used where the therapist provides a variety of toys, encourages the patient to play and may interpret some of his activities to him, if they seem to symbolize attitudes or feelings.

Counselling

Again this usually involves a one-to-one relationship of professional worker and client. Here the aim is usually to give a more practical kind of advice about personal, work or emotional problems.

Group discussions

Here a group of people meet regularly with one or more professional workers. As with reports on psychotherapy, many results are difficult to evaluate as little account is taken of intervening activities and criteria for claimed successes are vague. A particular aim of group discussion is to encourage co-operative behaviour within the group, like learning to listen to others and not to interrupt, and to encourage interactions within the group rather than each individual addressing the professional workers present.

Successes have been claimed in producing more outgoing behaviour and reducing withdrawn behaviour. One study (Synder and Sechrist 1959) which used a comparison group who did not participate in the group discussions demonstrated improvement in those who did by counting the increased number of positive comments on routine reports and the decreased number of appearances in behaviour courts for more serious violations (the subjects here were retarded delinquents).

Environmental therapy

Another approach to the treatment of disturbed behaviour, as an alternative to direct therapeutic methods, is to alter the disturbed person's surroundings. This method is more likely to be used with the severely handicapped person who is less likely to benefit from psychotherapy. Environmental change may involve a change of place of work, a move from home for a period in hospital, or a move to live in another ward in a hospital. The concept of environmental therapy covers all attempts made within a residential institution to make the environment conducive to adjusted behaviour and the maximum development of the resident. This would include provisions like partitioning wards to increase privacy, providing toys, books and games, decorating and providing attractive curtains, carpets and pictures, and encouraging outings and social activities.

Behaviour therapy
In recent years, principles taken from learning theory have been introduced to modify undesirable behaviour. Basically, the treatment involves ensuring that desired behaviour is immediately and appropriately rewarded and that undesired behaviour is not rewarded. For example, if a child rushes round a room, pushing over furniture and throwing movable articles around, he is rewarded during periods when he is sitting quietly and not rewarded or punished when he is being destructive. If an older person refuses to go to the table to eat a meal, he is not rewarded by attention being paid to him as this would be rewarding undesired behaviour. If he does not go to the table, he is deprived of the reward of food and has to go hungry until the next meal. (Such treatment is carried out with close medical supervision of the patient's condition.)

Rewards which are used or of which the subject of the treatment is deprived are of several kinds. They may be material rewards like food, sweets, money, toys for children, or they may be social, like attention or praise. Anything which is rewarding can be used as long as it is rewarding to the subject at that time and is given immediately following the desired behaviour. Undesired behaviour can be followed either by no reward or by punishment, though use of punishments is generally felt less desirable by those working with the handicapped and there are few cases where actual punishment is necessary.

It is sometimes convenient to use a token to represent a reward; tokens are generally round metal discs which are more convenient to handle than material rewards and avoid problems of satiation which can occur with frequent use of rewards like food.

Illustrations of the use of several of these techniques occur in an experimental study by Burchard and Barrera (1972).

Their experiment was carried out within a token economy system designed for rehabilitation of mildly retarded adolescent boys who displayed a high frequency of antisocial behaviour. Within the token system, tokens were mostly earned through achievement in the workshop and were exchanged for meals, privileges, clothes, recreational trips, or various purchases. A timeout procedure was introduced where the boys went to sit on a bench behind a partition, hence having timeout from being able to receive reinforcers (tokens); also a response-cost procedure where reinforcers were removed, that is tokens were taken away from the boys. Timeout and deprivation of tokens occurred following swearing, personal assault, property damage or other undesirable behaviour. They found that timeout and response-cost were as effective as each other in suppressing undesirable behaviour but the boys responded differently to different amounts of each. For five of six boys studied, thirty minutes timeout or thirty tokens taken away were more effective in reducing undesirable behaviour than five minutes timeout or five tokens removed. For the sixth boy, the lower values were more effective than the higher ones.

Behaviour modification techniques are being applied to a whole variety of what are traditionally considered disturbed behaviours with good results, the main practical difficulties being to find suitable reinforcers and to apply the techniques consistently. Critics have suggested that behaviour modification may succeed in changing specific behaviours but not the processes which underlie them, and also that it could be used to teach that behaviour which best fits in with the demands of the institution rather than that which is in the individual's best interests. However, much of the behaviour that is currently being taught is behaviour which is relevant to independent living in any situation.

7
Pychological assessment of the handicapped

In earlier chapters we mentioned some of the ways in which personality and educational attainment can be assessed. Here we shall examine how cognitive, developmental and behavioural levels are examined.

Reasons for assessment

There are two basic reasons for any assessment. Firstly, we are aiming at measuring a person's abilities in any one area; we may be assessing his IQ to determine if he is mentally handicapped, his speech level to see if he is retarded in that area or an aspect of his behaviour to see if it changes under different conditions. We are doing this in order to make predictions for the future about what kind of training he will need, and what level he is likely to achieve. Secondly, we assess a person to discover if he is changing, whether he is developing, staying at the same level or perhaps regressing, and whether he has strengths and weaknesses in his abilities, areas which are well developed or areas which are more retarded than his general level of development.

Proposals for assessment

It is now generally agreed that assessment of a handicapped person should be both multi-disciplinary and regular.

By multi-disciplinary we mean that a variety of specialists should be involved. Doctors, psychologists, social workers, speech therapists, teacher, physiotherapists, and several other professional workers all have a contribution to make to the assessment of the handicapped person.

Secondly, assessment should be regular. Development of ability in any one area is not necessarily even; at times the person will develop a skill more rapidly, at others he will progress slowly. In terms of general mental level, most children will remain at a roughly similar level in relation to their actual age, but some changes will occur. Occasionally there are dramatic alterations, usually due to changes in the environment or to discovery and correction of a condition which was retarding the individual. Regular reassessment will detect areas where he is falling behind and give an opportunity for special attention to be given to the area of deficit. Also, there are more difficulties involved in assessing a handicapped person than in assessing a non-handicapped one, if he has limited ways of making responses and fewer ways of taking in information. Regular reassessment will confirm whether accurate measures were made on previous occasions, or whether any ability was under-estimated.

Framework of assessment

If we are discussing strengths and weakness, area of retardation or of comparative deficit, we need to be able to say in relation to what. Four kinds of standard are commonly used the first two of which we discussed in the chapter on cognitive deficits.

1. *IQ as a standard*. An Intelligence Quotient or IQ describes a person's level of intelligence in relation to the rest of his age group and relates to the proportion of people of his own age who score higher and lower on the particular test being used. Similar quotients are used to describe other areas, such as Developmental Quotient, Social Quotient or Language Quotient. Quotients are most useful in describing attainments which are mildly impaired, but more difficult to use when scores are widely different from normal. On the most common scoring system, quotients below fifty-five relate to the scores of an extremely small percentage of the population, 0·14 per cent. Hence lower quotients than this of thirty or twenty relate, in percentage terms, to such a small proportion of the normal population that they mean very little; all they tell us is that a person with an IQ of thirty scored more than a person with an

IQ of twenty. For this reason mental ages are easier to use in assessing the severely handicapped.

2. *Mental age as a standard.* In this case, we relate a person's attainments in any one area to those of the average child in a particular age group, and say that his score on a test is equal to the score of half of the children of that age. Similarly, we can use Language Ages, Social Ages, Developmental Ages of various kinds. We are, however, only using an age scale as a convenient standard; to say that a child has a language age of three, for example, only describes his score on a particular test.

3. *Other handicapped people as a standard.* Occasionally other handicapped people are used as a standard for comparison and in this case scores on a test can tell us if a particular person is developing as well as the average handicapped person, or is below the level of most others. An advantage of this kind of standard is that it gives more attainable goals. The severely handicapped person is so far away from normality that achievement of average attainments would be impossible; aiming at an average level for handicapped people is more realistic.

4. *The person as his own standard.* In some assessment situations, what the rest of the population achieves is of little interest; we can compare the handicapped person's performance in different situations, for example, or when he is being rewarded in various ways. The only standard needed then is what the person himself achieves.

Methods of assessment

The particular method used in an assessment situation depends on the available responses of the person being assessed and the reasons why the assessment is being made.

Psychometric methods
Psychometric methods of assessment measure the subject's skills in a particular area of ability by giving him a predetermined standard set of questions to be answered or tasks to perform. His score is then compared with the norms of the test, the scores of a large group of people who were tested when the test was produced. A psychometric test must always be given in the prescribed way, otherwise comparison with the norms is pointless. The examiner is not allowed to alter the questions, to prompt the answers, to give clues or to help the

subject in any way that is not allowed for in the test instructions, as the subjects in the standardization group did not have this help.

Psychometric tests are mostly used to measure intelligence or various aspects of it. The particular choice of test to use with any handicapped individual depends both on the ways in which it can be explained to him what he has to do and on the ways in which he can respond. If the subject can hear and understand instructions, verbal explanations are usually used; if he cannot, mime has to be used to explain what is required. If he can speak, see and is not too physically handicapped, any method of response can be used; if he cannot speak, or his speech is so poor that the examiner cannot understand it, testing has to rely on pointing or non-verbal tasks like constructional items; if he cannot see, testing is through verbal response. Severely physically handicapped people can be tested verbally if their hearing and speech is adequate. Otherwise some indication of yes or no, or pointing if he can point reasonably accurately, is used. The most physically handicapped people may need to be assessed using nodding or shaking the head, to indicate response. Eye pointing can be used where no other response is available; objects used in the testing are spread well apart and the response is made by the subject looking at a particular object.

Tests used with the handicapped
Descriptions of a few of the tests used with handicapped people illustrate the methods of testing available. Some are designed to produce a general, overall intelligence quotient or mental age, others assess a particular area of functioning.

Hiskey Nebraska Test of Learning Aptitude. This test is designed for use with deaf or hearing children, and there are two sets of instructions, one using verbal requests, the other using mime; the verbal requests are, however, fairly simple. No verbal response is required from the subject but he performs various kinds of activity: threading beads of different shapes to copy patterns; pointing to the correct colour or colours from a series of different coloured strips of wood after the examiner has shown him the right colours, then hidden them; showing which of four pictures fits in with the concept e.g. toys exemplified in a set of three. As the test involves little or no verbal interaction, it can be used in assessing deaf people, or those whose language is impaired or considerably below the level of their non-verbal abilities.

Ravens Progressive Matrices. Comparative ease of explanation and simplicity of response are advantages here. The test consists of a booklet and each page contains an item. At the top of the page is a rectangle containing a pattern or symbols and one part of the design or sequence is missing; below are several alternative pieces which could fit into the rectangle but only one piece will correctly complete the design or sequence of symbols. Although the test should be explained verbally, it can be easily explained by mime, and if the person is intelligent enough to score on the test he readily understands the task. Answers to the test can be written, as each alternative has a number, or the subject can point to indicate his response. If accurate pointing is impossible, the examiner can point to each answer in turn and the subject can nod or shake his head. This latter method is less desirable as it departs from the original way of giving the test and makes the norms not strictly applicable, but in some cases nodding or shaking the head may be the only response available. There are adult and children's versions of this test and it can be used with physically handicapped people of normal levels of intelligence, but is too difficult for the mentally handicapped.

Peabody Picture Vocabulary Test. This is an easier test, which can be used in a similar way to the last test though the subject must be able to hear and understand speech as it aims to measure mental age through understanding of spoken words. Four pictures are presented; the examiner asks 'Which one is . . .?' and the subject indicates the appropriate picture. Again, this type of method can be used with subjects whose physical responses are limited.

Reynell Developmental Language Scale. This test is still in an experimental form but has proved useful in assessing the handicapped whose language levels are below six years. Expressive speech is assessed using a series of questions about displayed toys. Comprehension can be assessed in two ways. If the child has reasonable motor control, he points to or moves the toys in accordance with instructions; there is, however, a special scale for use with the severely physically handicapped, where response can be made by the eye-pointing method mentioned previously.

These four tests indicate some of the ways in which psychometric tests can be used with handicapped children. Of course, many handicapped children whose handicaps are not too severe can be given the same kinds of test as any other child. It is usually the more severe handicaps which need special selection of tests.

In general, the choice of test depends less on the diagnostic grouping of the child and more on the individual's actual available responses. Tests of the kind described above are usually used to obtain a general measure of the person's level, to know if he is retarded and to what extent, to help to decide what kind of education he needs or what kind of understanding he has.

Experimental assessments

Sometimes we do not need a test but are more interested in planning an assessment to answer an individual problem. We may want to discover under what conditions an individual works best. We could devise a series of tasks for him which he performs, perhaps alone and then in a noisy, crowded room. We may want to know if he is benefiting from a hearing aid or glasses, and give him the same set of questions or visual discrimination puzzles with and without the aid. Sometimes a person who seems to be capable of some responses is unable to co-operate on testing or cannot respond correctly to the easiest items; we then need to try various tasks in the hope of discovering what the subject can and will do, so that we can determine why these tasks differed from the test. This kind of assessment tells us nothing about whether the person is retarded, or how he performs in relation to the rest of the population, but helps us to suggest how he can best be trained.

Learning assessments

The use of tests has sometimes been criticized because the results tell us only what the child has learned in the past and not what he is capable of learning. He may have had fewer opportunities for learning and given the right conditions may be able to learn much faster in the future. Another approach to assessment, then, is to teach the child something in the assessment situation. At a very simple level it may be to point to a picture of a ball on each occasion when two pictures are presented with the order randomly reversed. At a more complicated level, it may be to match a series of shapes to a model as quickly as possible. Whereas in a test, a particular task is given only once, or occasionally two or three times, and the subject is recorded as passing or failing, in a learning assessment he is given the task as many times as he needs to succeed or until we can get a useful measure of the rate at which he learns. There are no extensive norms available for this kind of assessment at present, so again we cannot say how his learning compares with his age group or with that of a large group of the non-handicapped, but we can learn more about him as an individual in terms of how quickly he learns, and whether he reaches his maximum level quickly or slowly. A learning assessment can be used to investigate what kind of reinforcements are effective for an individual. He could be taught one task, perhaps to match three shapes correctly by being given a sweet every time he was successful; he could then be taught to match three different shapes by being praised for success. This process would be repeated several times, varying the shapes and the order in which each reinforcer is used to avoid the effects of practice; we could then discover which of the reinforcers was most effective for him.

Assessment by observation
Some handicapped children are too handicapped or too disturbed to co-operate in a psychometric test, or on the kind of task which may be used in a test. Alternative methods of assessment are then needed. One way is to observe the child's everyday activities and to use some kind of developmental scale as a standard by which to reach a measure of his level. Sometimes his sensori-motor progress can be assessed in this way; this is a useful measure of development as the kind of behaviour involved is essential for later progress (see C2). Toys are given to the child and the examiner encourages him to play in such a way as to indicate which stage of development he has reached. Holding out a toy to him is used to assess if he can grasp objects; hiding the toy and encouraging him to find it indicates whether he knows that objects continue to exist when he cannot see them; simple problem-solving, like pulling a string or using a rake to obtain a desired object, again suggests his level of sensori-motor development. The objects used can be varied according to the child's interests and sweets or

biscuits can be used for hiding and problem-solving if these produce more response. The kinds of play reactions observed can then be related to the age that the normal child achieves each one and an approximate developmental level determined.

Observation is also used in assessing day to day behaviour. Although tests are comparatively rapid and uncomplicated to use, the tasks involved are often not important in themselves and are only used as measures of the general concept of intelligence. Moreover, we do not always want to know about a person's levels of development, but may be more interested in his daily behaviour or his particular behaviour problems.

In this type of observation, we are concerned with objectivity and measurement. When being objective, we avoid observations like 'he became angry' or 'he was bored' as these are our interpretations of his feelings and we could be mistaken. We aim rather at describing the actual behaviour that occurs such as 'throwing himself to the ground and drumming his heels' or 'sitting by the window, looking outwards, not moving'. By measurement, we can improve on statements like 'he often does . . .' or 'he rarely . . .' by counting events – such as kicking other people or spitting – or by measuring the length of time a piece of behaviour lasts – such as a period of sitting or time spent looking at a magazine.

By observing behaviours, situations and sequences of behaviour, we can make suggestions about what precedes undesirable behaviour, where and in what circumstances it happens, what the consequences usually are and hence how it might be altered.

Assessment by interview with others

In some cases, particularly if the child is in a strange place and reacting badly or if he is too withdrawn to be approached, the most satisfactory way of assessing him is to interview persons who know him well, and use the information they give. In the case of a person living at home, a parent or relative is usually interviewed; for a child in a residential placement, a nurse, housemother or teacher gives the information. The most often-used scale in this situation is the Vineland Social Maturity Scale. This consists of items concerned with daily living skills at the younger age levels and with aspects of participating in the community at older ones, like using mail order, going shopping, taking part in community life. The scale is rarely used in the upper levels as the items are felt to be class-biased and more dependent on interest than maturity but at the lower levels it involves the more universal areas of development, like speech development, feeding, dressing and toilet training. The scale is completed by the examiner asking the informant what the child does in each area of development and scoring each item accordingly. The scores from the scale are converted to Social Quotients and Social Ages but have quite close relationship to Intelligence Quotients and Mental Ages at the lower age levels.

Assessment by others

Psychologists now feel that they need not always do assessment themselves but can usefully produce methods to be used by others.

Experimental use has been made of assessment by parents in this context. This produces a measure of the child's development but, more importantly, is of value to the parents in helping them to learn more about their child, to be realistic about him and to see areas of delay which could be remedied. Several studies have shown that parents tend to overestimate their child's abilities, particularly when the child is physically handicapped and of low intelligence. This overestimation is undesirable if it means that parents' aspirations for the future are too high and that they will be eventually disillusioned; and if they fail to provide the most stimulating environment for their child that they can by misunderstanding his level of comprehension and his ability to participate. If the parents have a developmental scale to complete, they are encouraged to observe their child in a much more objective fashion.

An assessment scale in use by teachers, nurses and workshop supervisors and others directly involved with the handicapped is Gunzberg's Progress Assessment Charts. These charts are designed for assessment and regular reassessment of the attainments of mentally handicapped people in four basic areas: in Communication, where the extent of understanding and verbal expression is assessed; Socialization, which includes the development of interaction with other people; Self-Help in walking, feeding, dressing and generally becoming independent; and in Occupation which assesses skills learned. Standards of attainment in these areas by other mentally handicapped people are available and the recording chart is designed to highlight areas of comparative deficit.

Some problems of assessment of the handicapped

Most of the problems we shall raise here refer to the use of psychometric tests with the handicapped. Parents are sometimes unhappy about psychological assessment sessions where tests are used. The reasons for this may stem, in some cases, from the parent and the psychologist having different aims. The psychologist is aiming at an accurate realistic measure of the child's abilities so as to produce valid information. The parent is much more likely to see the situation in terms of passing and failing, wants the child to do as well as possible and is often hoping that the results will prove that the child is less handicapped than was previously thought.

An objection that often arises is that when the assessment was made, the child was reacting badly to being in a strange place with a strange person, and so was not doing as well as he could. Watching a child being tested can be a frustrating experience for a parent or teacher who knows how differently the child reacts under familiar conditions. However, the criticism that assessment is unfair when done in unfamiliar surroundings is not always justified. In using a psychometric test we are comparing any one child's performance with that of the large number of children who were tested when the test was produced. This group of children was also tested under unfamiliar conditions, though they were in many cases non-handicapped. So the test is unfair to, or invalid for, the particular handicapped child only if he reacts more than is normal to strange surroundings and this will vary with the individual child. Some handicapped children are unworried by strange surroundings, some seem to do better with a person they do not know and enjoy a situation where they are the centre of attention and are being praised for good performance. Only when a handicapped child has little experience of new places, is very shy or resists trying tasks through fear of failure is there a risk that the test will underestimate his abilities. When this kind of under-performing is suspected, it is best to assess the child at home or to base assessment on an interview with someone who knows him well.

Another objection sometimes raised is that tests can include content which is less familiar to the handicapped child, particularly if he lives in a hospital. Even if he lives at home, he may be less familiar with everyday objects than a more mobile child, and know less about railway trains, shops, cooking, animals and games. A child who lives in hospital is likely to be more restricted in experience and less familiar with items involving an ordinary home life, too. It is very likely that the handicapped child is at a disadvantage on many tests for this reason. However, when we are using a test, we are measuring intelligence, or language as it is at that time, regardless of the reasons why it is at that level. Any child's test performance is a product of many factors, including his experience, and this will reflect in the test result. We cannot modify a particular test to avoid possible disadvantages to any individual child, this would make use of the test pointless as we could not compare the score with the norms. The solution is to use several tests and to select those which are least obviously affected by experience.

A further reason for using several tests, rather than a single one, to make an assessment is that tests are not absolutely reliable. If a child were tested every day for several days, IQs from the tests would vary within a range of about ten IQ points. For an occasional individual, the most reliable test can produce wider differences on different occasions. When an important decision is to be made affecting the handicapped child, and based on the result of the test, this variability needs to be taken into account.

In fact, if several tests are used, a better description of the subject's abilities can be given. If an overall IQ or mental age estimate is needed, a test which involves many types of item is given. Within these types of item, there is a whole range of patterns of passes and failures which can add up to the same end result. A single IQ or mental age tells us very little about what the subject can actually do, where he needs extra help and where he is doing well. If a combination of tests is used, we can learn more about the individual's pattern of abilities and compare, for example, his understanding of language, his expressive language, his social development and his non-verbal level.

A final problem arising in use of psychometric tests with the handicapped arises when the subject has very few responses, and test items that can be answered by nodding or pointing are used. When the test materials are spread out between the examiner and the subject it is difficult for the examiner to avoid looking at the correct response and giving the subject clues as to which is the right answer. Particularly difficult is the answer method where the examiner says 'Is it this one?' to each item and the subject nods or shakes his head, as voice inflections can indicate an expectation of the answer. An examiner needs to be sure his behaviour is very controlled and, for similar reasons, if another person is present they need to be seated well away from the testing table or behind the subject.

A general point which arises when assessment is being carried out by interviewing someone about the handicapped person, is that questions should always be framed in terms of what the person regularly does and not what he can do. The latter phrasing has been found to produce over-estimates when the question is answered on the grounds that he could do a certain thing were he not too handicapped.

Classification by adaptive behaviour

Traditionally, most concepts and definitions of mental handicap include the presence of below-normal intelligence, and much emphasis has been placed on the results of intelligence testing. Although for many years interest had been shown in the social and adaptive aspects of behaviour, the concept of using levels of behaviour as a classification only came into prominence in 1959. The American Association on Mental Deficiency suggested that the behavioural classification of mental retardation should include two dimensions: measured intelligence and adaptive behaviour. These two dimensions were seen as closely related in most cases but sufficiently different in some to warrant the inclusion of both dimensions in the definition. That is, though most people of retarded intelligence would also show poor adaptive behaviour levels, a few may have low intelligence but good adaptive behaviour and a few may have the reverse. Adaptive behaviour is seen as the ability to cope with the natural and social demands of the environment, that is, the degree to which an individual can maintain himself independently in the community and his ability to behave in a manner consistent with the established norms of personal behaviour.

Classification of adaptive behaviour is in terms of five levels, ranging from no impairment, through mild negative deviation, moderate and severe, to profound negative deviation. Initially classification was based largely on judgement, but scales have since been produced to measure adaptive behaviour and are in process of being further developed.

The Adaptive Behaviour Scales consist of two parts, one designed for use with children aged three to twelve, the other for people aged thirteen years upwards to adult level. There are two parts to each scale; the first assesses performance in what are referred to as the domains of independent functioning – physical development, economic activities, language development, number and time concepts, occupation-domestic, occupation-general, self-direction, responsibility, and socialization. The second part is concerned with the domains of violent and destructive behaviour, antisocial behaviour, rebellious behaviour, untrustworthy behaviour, withdrawal, stereotyped behaviour and odd mannerisms, inappropriate interpersonal manners, unacceptable vocal habits, unacceptable or eccentric habits, self-abusive behaviour, hyperactive tendencies, sexually aberrant behaviour, psychological disturbances and the use of medication.

Although it is generally agreed that these areas of adaptive behaviour are important, there is disagreement as to whether the concept should be used as part of or as the entire definition of mental retardation, in addition to or in preference to a definition based on retarded intelligence.

Arguments in favour of using adaptive behaviour in classification and definition are based on two main points. First, since we now regard helping the retarded to become integrated into the community, rather than segregating them, as being of prime importance, the real needs of the mentally handicapped will be neglected until adaptability is made a central issue. And second, although it is possible that more people are included within the definition of 'mentally retarded' when the adaptive behaviour classification is added, those who are unable to function in a tolerable manner or to be accepted by their society will become noticeable in any case and will need special help and provisions made for them, regardless of their IQ. It has also been commented that the concept of behaviourally maladapted involves more implications for training, for it is less easy to see what to teach a class of 'retarded children' than it is to have ideas for teaching children defined as not adapted to the surroundings, as in the latter case the deficit is more specifically defined and some standard to aim at is available.

Against fundamental use of the concept are the following arguments. The idea of adaptive behaviour is vague and ill-defined as compared with the psychometric definition, and is somewhat subjective in its application. The use of a maladaptive behaviour definition includes those who choose not to adapt but are clearly not mentally retarded, and the inclusion of all those who are not adapted would result in a large mixed group of 'non-normals' with many varying characteristics, whereas to progress, we should be refining classification and subdivisions for research in treatment and training. To assess adaptive behaviour we need assessments both of the individual and of the relevant community, as ease of adaption must vary. Maladaptive behaviour is generally seen as reversible by training, which makes it difficult to use as part of a definition. For all these reasons, the argument goes, limited intelligence should remain the core characteristic of what we call mental retardation, and although intellectual impairment tends to result in poor adaptive behaviour, the latter concept should not be made central and part of the definition of mental retardation.

8
Educational and early training aspects

In this chapter we shall discuss a few of the methods which have been used to increase the levels of attainment of handicapped children.

Early intervention

It is now generally felt that training for the handicapped should begin as early as possible, for as we saw in earlier chapters, every handicapped child is likely to have fewer experiences than normal because of the limitations of his handicap and it is difficult for a mother to compensate for all these limitations without assistance. Early intervention is particularly desirable if the child's home background is unsatisfactory in any way, for there is a risk that, if no early help is given, the child will already be backward – especially in cognitive areas like language and reasoning – by the time he goes to school.

Current trends are towards providing early help in two basic ways; provision of early educational facilities in the form of a class or nursery group and assistance to mothers to help them train their children. Early intervention programmes have been based on either of these methods or a combination of both.

Direct help to mothers has been felt to be important as in some cases they have problems themselves and may not be capable of providing the child with adequate stimulation and necessary experiences. In addition, assistance for most mothers of handicapped children is valuable as they tend to be deprived of the help of friends and neighbours in knowing what games to play with the child, and how to talk to him. The mother of a normal small child usually knows several other mothers and has experience of how they behave to their children. A mother of a handicapped child is less likely to know another mother in the same situation and so is deprived of some opportunities to share ideas and experiences. A third advantage of providing direct help to mothers is that the effects are lasting and even if the actual programme is short, the ideas and methods learned are likely to be applied for a much longer time. There is some evidence that gains in the child's level during a programme where the mother is involved are maintained for longer than those where the programme has been carried out away from the home only.

It has been found, however, that advice to mothers needs to be fairly specific. Vague recommendations, like 'stimulate him' or 'talk to him as often as possible', are less effective than definite suggestions of what games to play, how to play them, what situations to teach language in and how to teach it.

Programmes for mothers and activities in nursery groups have the same basic aims; they try to structure and guide the child's activities so that he has experiences that he can understand, and so that he has as many of the experiences of a non-handicapped child as possible in order to try and avoid secondary handicaps through lack of relevant activity.

Advantages of nursery group provision are particularly important if the child's home experiences are restricted by difficulties in keeping him occupied and in taking him out, or if his mother has little time to spend with him. The positive aspects of this kind of provision are that the child has access to companions; that to go to another place during the day provides him with a change of environment and a journey that he usually enjoys. The nursery group will usually provide him with a wider variety of play equipment than most homes can provide and often more space and more opportunity to be untidy. In addition, attending nursery group has been felt to lessen the child's dependence on the mother and helps him to accept other adults, and also lessens the mother's dependence on the child as, particularly with a handicapped child, a mother can sometimes focus all her interests on him to the exclusion of her friends, interests and the rest of the family.

It has been suggested too that a pre-school group provides valuable opportunities for early essential learning specific to some handicaps; for example, one programme included deaf children in a normal pre-school group and the deaf children were taught to use their hearing aids correctly, and were encouraged to interact verbally with the other children, to develop communication with them, and they were taught to listen as is so often necessary with deaf children.

Some disadvantages of the nursery groups for the handicapped have been raised. It has been felt that in some cases the child receives less attention that he would at home, though this depends, of course, on how much time his mother has available and whether there are young children present with competing demands. It has also been suggested that there is a risk that he will copy undesirable behaviour from other children, particularly if he sees that their behaviour attracts attention. A third disadvantage has been felt to be that there are many levels of handicap and that the more advanced child's development may be influenced by the more retarded ones.

In general, it has been found necessary to balance the advantages and disadvantages for any particular child, and where it has been possible to arrange for a handicapped child to attend a normal nursery school most of the suggested disadvantages are avoided. Whether this is possible has depended to a large extent on the degree of the child's handicap and whether he is able to participate in a reasonable number of activities.

Early intervention in subcultural mental handicap
Much attention has been paid in recent years to the possibility of ameliorating or preventing some children from becoming mentally retarded by the introduction of early training. It is known that mothers within the IQ range of about forty to eighty tend to produce a high proportion of children with similarly low IQs. To some extent, this may be the effect of genetic inheritance, but it is likely that it is also due to the mother's inability to provide an adequate early upbringing for the child. The term 'subcultural' refers to mental retardation which is due to poor cultural background.

Attempts to intervene in the process and prevent subcultural retardation have been made in America, and many of the programmes introduced showed gains in the participating children's development at the time of the programme, though these gains were often small and tended not to be maintained after the special programme had ended.

Various programmes have been used, usually including a

pre-school group and home involvement. School attendance varied from full-time to half-time and home involvement was either in the form of a parents' meeting or a weekly home visit by a professional adviser. Many of these programmes have since been felt inadequate on the grounds that they were often rather short and introduced too late; by the time the child entered the programme at two or three years old, he was already retarded and could not both remedy his deficits and continue to progress rapidly enough to achieve a normal level when he reached school age. In many of the programmes there was no provision made to follow up special pre-school teaching into school and to reinforce earlier learning, so any gains which had been made were lost again in a year or two. Thirdly, the programmes used for teaching in the pre-school classes were often unstructured and designed to give the child a wide range of experiences, largely through exploration and free activity; it seems likely however that learning through one's own exploring and experimenting is just what these children had not learned to do and that they needed a much more structured programme where defined and planned activities were directly taught, and that they needed direct teaching in a narrower range of important areas like language and reasoning rather than a widely-based programme.

Studies using nursery school methods of free activity and free play generally showed some benefit to the child at the time and small IQ gains occurred, but they were generally less than ten IQ points. When special cognitive training was added to the nursery school programme slightly greater gains occurred and some studies which extended the programme to include sessions of training in the child's home produced IQ gains in some cases of up to twenty points. However, the deficit of the children participating was only partly remedied in every case and no group reached an average IQ level. When the programme of intervention ceased and the children went to school, gains were lost in a fairly short time. In general, the children who had the lowest IQs at the beginning of the programme, those who were youngest and those from families who volunteered participation, made the greatest gains. Where the deprivation in the family was least, the gains lasted longest but rarely for more than a year or two. When emphasis was on the home and the mother was encouraged to use books and toys and interact with the child, IQ gains lasted longer but rarely exceeded twenty points and did not generally succeed in bringing most children to average level.

It seems that these programmes, though having some influence on the children's development, were not adequate to compensate for the deprivation that probably affected them from their early weeks in every sphere of development.

An intervention on a much larger scale is now being carried out in Milwaukee by Heber *et al.* (1972), and early results are promising. The project is being carried out with forty low-income families where the mother's IQ is less than seventy-five and where there was a new-born child at the time the project was begun. These families were divided into an experimental group, and a control group for comparison where no intervention took place.

The programme for the experimental group involved both the mothers and the children. The mothers were given help by the provision of care for any other pre-school children during the day. They spent four weeks in full-time education in reading, writing, various aspects of running a home and home economics, and in child care. They then worked for twenty-six weeks in a nursing home under supervision; there they learned housework, laundry, cooking and simple nursing and after this period found full-time employment.

The babies attended a Special Infant Education Centre and were given an intensive programme of sensory and language stimulation. Each baby had his own teacher and in the first year there was one adult available for every child; after the first year the adult to child ratio was one to three. The programmes provided were very detailed and covered the areas of cognitive, motor and language development.

The babies in the experiment and the babies not included were regularly assessed and little difference between the groups was apparent until they were fourteen months old. However, after that, the experimental group developed at a much faster rate and by five years there were wide differences. The average IQ for the experimental group was 124, whereas the control group average was thirty points less. Moreover, in language development there was a difference between the groups of twelve to eighteen months. Measures of the verbal interaction between mother and child showed that although they had spent less time together, their interaction was on a better developed level than that of the control group. It is not yet known whether the effects of the early intervention will continue as the children grow older but it seems that major and extensive assistance during the early years is likely to be more effective than the more limited programme.

School placement

When the handicapped child goes to school, he will either prove to be able to cope with normal education or it will be necessary to make special educational provision for him (see C4). He may need full-time normal education or full-time special education, though between these there are several other possible arrangements.

Special schools may be fully residential, pupils may be resident during the week only or they may attend daily from home. In some instances, a handicapped child can attend a normal school for some parts of the week and a special school for the rest. Increasingly, handicapped pupils are attending special classes in normal schools. Where any particular child attends school tends to depend on the provisions available, the facilities of the schools and the degree of the child's handicap, as it is usually easier to incorporate a mildly handicapped child into a normal school than a severely handicapped one.

Various attempts have been made to determine whether particular groups of children are better placed in normal or special schools but results have been inconsistent and conclusions vary.

Arguments for handicapped children attending normal schools include the point that as the handicapped child will at some stage be likely to have to come to terms with the real, non-handicapped world, it is better to keep him in it and not segregate him with his own handicap group. The presence of handicapped children in the school will also familiarize the other children with handicaps and their implications. It has been feared, however, that a handicapped child in a normal school may be isolated and rejected by his peers, particularly if he has physical problems which are unacceptable to the other children. For example, doubts have been expressed as to whether those children with spina bifida who are incontinent would be happy in a normal class, as the incontinence might cause the other children to reject them. However, a study of the adjustment of school children with spina bifida – one group of whom were incontinent and one group of whom were not – showed that there were no differences between them. It seems to have been common experience, at least with younger children, that there are no noticeable problems in other children's reactions to the incontinence.

Advantages of special schools for the handicapped have been seen in terms of the possibilities for arranging the entire school programme, equipment and buildings to meet the special needs of the particular handicap group. The main disadvantage, apart from the possibility that being educated with his own handicap group only may make the handicapped child's adjustment more difficult on leaving school, refers in particular to special schools for the educationally subnormal. It is felt that a certain stigma is attached to attending an ESN school which may affect the child both when he is at school and afterwards, and he may resist telling anyone that he went to a special school.

This may be a problem for only a few pupils, however. One survey of the attitudes of pupils looking back on their schooling two years after they left found that only a few showed an awareness of stigma. Twenty-five young people who had attended special school for the educationally subnormal were interviewed, and although only four were unreservedly appreciative and three were moderately enthusiastic (there were no comparable figures for leavers from normal schools), only four expressed an awareness of any stigma. This took the form of, for example, never telling employees or colleagues where they had been to school.

Comparisons of achievements and integration of children in normal classes, special classes in normal schools and in special schools have been complicated by the existence in many cases of selection factors which mean that those in normal schools were less handicapped before they began their education. When these differences are adequately allowed for, differences in school achievement are very small, though there has been a suggestion that the social adjustment of mentally retarded children in special classes is better than that of those in normal classes, the latter can be isolated or rejected.

When handicapped children are educated in normal schools it is important that the teacher is involved and fully informed so that she can cope with any problems arising, such as dealing with hearing aids and ensuring that they are working, coping with fits in the classroom or placing the child so that he can see and hear adequately.

That teachers are not always informed of handicaps is clear from Bagley's (1971) study of epileptic children. The teachers of 109 children responded to a general questionnaire about the child's health and any physical disabilities he had. Only forty-three of the teachers showed an indication in their responses that they were aware that the child had epilepsy; the remaining sixty-six gave no indication that they knew, even though many of them gave very detailed responses about the child's health and behaviour. In some cases, the information would clearly have helped in their understanding of the child – as in the case of one teacher who commented that a boy had poor concentration, when she did not know that he had one or two petit mal attacks in a day. In many cases, Bagley found that the school underestimated intelligence level when the child's IQ was high but his reading and/or his arithmetic was retarded.

The teacher not only needs to be informed of relevant handicaps, but must also understand the condition and its implications. In the case of epilepsy, Bagley points out that adverse factors in the school environment – for instance, a teacher's hostility, or over-anxiety, being over-excluded from activities by the teacher, or a rejecting attitude of other children – can make both behaviour and fits worse. Teachers can, however, facilitate adjustment by providing an understanding, non-alarmist attitude if the child has a fit.

Behaviour modification in schools for the handicapped

In recent years the techniques of behaviour modification – as described in pp. 92–93 – in relation to disturbed behaviour, have been applied in classroom settings, mainly within normal classes and in classes for the mentally handicapped. Academic performance and social behaviour have both been shown to improve if appropriate and immediate reinforcement is given for desired behaviours.

A variety of rewards has been used – including praise for good achievement or appropriate behaviour, edible reinforcers, some kind of token system, or a card which is ticked or has a star placed on it. The tokens, ticks or stars are usually exchanged at the end of the school day for sweets or toys and tend to be much more convenient systems to handle in the classroom.

Dalton *et al.* (1973) introduced a token economy system into the classroom to see if children with Down's Syndrome would improve in school subjects. The children were both male and female from six to fourteen years old, who lived at home and attended school daily. Their IQs on a non-verbal test ranged from thirty to sixty-four. Before the experiment began they were given tests of academic achievement; a language test was given, using a picture of a boy in bed with his eyes closed and asking questions like 'What is this?' pointing to the boy, 'Is this a boy?', 'Say the whole thing' (the child is expected to say 'this is a boy'), 'Is this a chair?' and so on up to nine questions; there was also an arithmetic test with items like counting to a certain number, counting how many times the examiner claps and identifying number symbols.

The children were divided into two groups. The group which was to receive tokens as rewards attended school in the mornings and the control group attended in the afternoons. Both were given the same teaching programme in language and in arithmetic according to a structured and clearly specified method where the instructor asks questions and the children answer. The differences between the groups was only in the use of tokens. All correct answers for both groups were praised but in the token group each child was given a token in addition to praise for approximately every fifth question he answered correctly. The children who received tokens exchanged them for sweets at the end of the session.

Classroom sessions were held three half-days a week for eight weeks and all the children were retested at the end of the programme. It was found that of the group which had received tokens every child except one had made gains on the arithmetic tests and all but one had increased their scores on the language test. In contrast only two of the control group increased their scores on the arithmetic test. However, all of the six control group children improved on the language test too, but when the children were retested on the same tests a year later, the group who had received tokens maintained the scores better than the group who had not; this latter group's score showed a decrease from the test immediately after the programme to the test a year later. The authors concluded that the results of a very short token economy programme could produce more lasting effects. They had also assessed the children's conduct during the programme to see if the incidence of undesirable classroom behaviour changed; they recorded incidents like making disruptive noise, aggression, disturbing others, but found the use of tokens for correct answers had had no effect on conduct.

A few studies have demonstrated the effects of behaviour modification techniques on social interaction in retarded children. It has often been commented that severely retarded children are inclined to play alone and not interact with adults or other children. Guralnick and Kravik (1973) demonstrated that a teacher and an assistant can develop social interactions in a classroom. The subjects of the study were eight severely retarded children aged six to ten years, none of whom could use intelligible words. The teacher and her assistant conducted the sessions for half an hour every weekday morning in the classroom and they were observed from an adjacent room through a one-way mirror.

Two kinds of activity were involved. Some sessions were spent in a group situation, where the children were encouraged to pass a brick to each other. These sessions were used to give reinforcement. Other sessions were used for free play to see if any effects carried over. Before the experiment was begun, the children's social behaviour was rated in terms of looking at or touching other children or the teachers and their non-social behaviour was recorded in terms of aggression, leaving the group or isolation. At this stage, it was found that social interactions were virtually non-existent in that on average they engaged in social behaviour for 2 per cent of the time. On the basis of their social behaviour scores they were divided into two groups, one of which received edible reinforcers during the experimental sessions and the other received social reinforcement only, when the teacher praised a child or patted him on the head. In addition, during the block-passing sessions, rewards were given at random on some occasions to see if it was important that reward followed immediately after the behaviour being encouraged, or whether giving sweets to the children during the session at random times increased their social behaviour in any case.

Results showed that when the group being given edible reinforcers were given them immediately following the desired social behaviours, the percentage of the time this group spent in social behaviour increased from around 2 per cent to 60 or 65 per cent over twelve sessions. When the sweets were given at random, social behaviour reduced markedly but increased again when the rewards were again made contingent on social behaviour. The changes were seen in all members of the group. The group who were reinforced with praise did not increase their social behaviour at all; they were later given edible reinforcers too and the same effect occurred as in the first group for three of the four children – their social behaviour increased. The fourth child was almost unchanged by the introduction of edible reinforcement. The increased social behaviour did not occur in the free play sessions where no reinforcement was given; during these, social behaviour remained unchanged.

It appeared that the social behaviour which was affected most by edible reinforcers was non-aggressive physical contact with both the teacher and other children, though various other behaviours occurred too. The authors feel that the emergence of these behaviours is an important step in developing meaningful social relationships.

Behaviour modification in early training

Similar techniques have been applied to early training in self-help skills, and in the case of some handicapped children slightly later training in the skills usually acquired in the first few years. Again, most work has been undertaken in the field of mental handicap but in a few cases the same techniques have been applied to the development of motor skills in children with cerebral palsy.

Marked increases in self-help skills can sometimes be achieved with appropriate intensive training. Colwell *et al.* (1973) describe a short-term residential institution for severely retarded children where success has been achieved using an intensive training and structured play routine. Their technique is to use positive tangible rewards like sweets, biscuits or soft drinks at first, and then, as training progresses, to introduce social praise as a reward and fade out use of the edible rewards. Training takes place over a fifteen-hour day in living quarters, the dining room, the playground and a training centre where motor skills and communication are taught. They describe results they have achieved in teaching feeding, dressing and toileting skills to forty-seven children who stayed in the institution for periods of between three and thirteen months. Their ages were between four and fifteen years and they were severely mentally handicapped, their IQs ranging from five to forty with an average of sixteen.

Although not all the children gained in scores on scales assessing dressing, feeding and toileting, the majority did;

forty-four of the forty-seven improved in dressing, thirty-six improved in feeding and thirty-three increased their scores on the toileting assessment scale. It proved possible to raise the average dressing level from being able, when told, to take off t-shirt, trousers, shoes and socks and possibly coat and beginning to learn to put on a t-shirt, which was the average level at the beginning of the training, to being able to dress and undress when each article of clothing was called by name. Feeding was raised from a level where a child could chew food, drink from a glass neatly, use a spoon only messily and eat bread with his hands to a level where he could do all these things neatly and use a fork efficiently too. The average toileting level at the beginning of training described a child who would go to the bathroom when told, but who needs help with his clothes and has accidents, whereas after training the average level was that of going on command, needing no help with clothes and having few if any accidents. These gains seem comparatively small in relation to the rate of development of these skills in a non-handicapped child but these children were severely retarded, and had developed very few skills to that time. This study did not use a control group but the authors felt that as the children had developed so few skills in the past, progress could reasonably be attributed to the training programme. They also found increases in mental age, as measured by intelligence tests over the period that the children received intensive training; the average level of mental age rose from 16·7 months to 20·1 months and the range of mental age in the group changed from a spread of seven to thirty-two months to nine to forty-one months. As the average stay was 7·1 months, these gains are impressive.

Another study which illustrates the improvement possible in the behaviour of severely handicapped children was undertaken at the Royal Scottish National Hospital (Tierney 1973), where a ward toilet-training programme was undertaken. It was observed that on the ward in question, 21·9 per cent of the nurses' activities were related to incontinence amongst the children and 17 per cent were related to toilet management. In the pre-experimental phase, 200 toileting episodes were observed in detail and each child's individual behaviour pattern noted. Two groups of eighteen patients were selected for the experiment; the two groups were of approximately the same age range (between six and twenty-one years), the same mental age range (between 4·2 and 22·6 months) and were similar in diagnosis, general level of functioning, degree of incontinence and degree of mobility. One group then underwent a special toilet-training programme whereas no alteration was made in the usual treatment of the second group which was used for comparison. Stages of training were planned, with the aim of finally teaching the patient to go to the toilet independently, to remove his clothing, to sit on the toilet and use it and to remain continent otherwise. For example, the 'going to the toilet' stages were: 'patient is taken to toilet by nurse', 'patient indicates his need to eliminate', 'patient asks to go to the toilet' and 'patient goes to the toilet independently'; each of these stages was aimed at in turn and when it was achieved the next stage was attempted. Similarly, stages were planned for coping with clothing, sitting and remaining continent.

During the programme, all appropriate toilet behaviour was reinforced, by rewarding the child with social approval and attention and a material reward such as sweets or toys depending on what the child liked. The programme continued for ninety days and at the end of that time fourteen of the eighteen patients had shown marked improvement, though none of them became completely trained in all aspects. However, in the ward as a whole, where there was a total of fifty-two patients, the number of observed episodes of incontinence was reduced from 177 in twenty-four hours in the pre-experimental phase to 148 in twenty-four hours in the post-experimental phase, and this decrease was attributable to the improved continence of the eighteen who had been trained.

The control group who had not received the reinforcement but continued to be toileted in traditional ways had changed very little. Later, the experimental programme was repeated with seventeen of these eighteen control group patients with very similar results and the ward incontinence episodes were then reduced to 116 in twenty-four hours. It was interesting to note that in the course of the experiment patients acquired skills in all areas of the Progress Assessment Chart which was used to assess them; self-help was expected to improve as it includes toilet training, but to a lesser extent communication, socialization and occupation all showed gains too, although they were not being directly taught.

Two examples of the use of operant techniques with children with cerebral palsy are quoted by Connolly (1968). Both were aimed at improving motor development. One involved the use of a game they had designed where the children had to respond by hitting a target. At first, the target is very large and the child is usually successful. Then a shaping technique is used where the speed and accuracy of the motor skill is gradually shaped by requiring the response to be made more rapidly and making the target gradually smaller. Successes were reinforced by a wide range of items.

The second demonstration of shaping motor development in a child with cerebral palsy was by Meyerson *et al.* (1967). In this case the subject was a seven-year-old boy diagnosed as mildly spastic with left hemiplegia who would not stand without something to hold on to and would not walk unless someone held his hand, although his doctor felt he was capable of doing so. It was felt that the boy was rewarded for this behaviour because he received attention on account of his handicap. He was thus rewarded with tokens, which could be exchanged for sweets and toys, at first if he moved his chair to the experimenter's desk to show him the results of the colouring task he was given, then for standing at the desk without holding on, then for turning from holding one chair back to hold another chair back behind him. The chairs were then moved further apart and within a fairly small number of sessions he was walking around the room.

Behaviour modification techniques are being applied to a wide range of developmental problems and seem generally effective, once a suitable reinforcement has been found for the particular child and as long as the reinforcement is applied consistently and immediately following the desired behaviour. Basic problems concern generalization and extinction (see A3). Will the learning generalize so that the child performs the desired behaviour in other different (but appropriate) situations? And will the child continue with the behaviour when the reward ceases to be provided by the psychologist or teacher? One solution to the latter problem is to teach behaviour which brings its own reward by bringing the environment more under the child's control (e.g. teaching him to ask for something or to perform skills which will bring approval).

9
Residential care for the handicapped

Mentally retarded people with and without other handicaps are the largest group of the handicapped who live away from their homes in residential care. A considerable number of the physically handicapped also live in residential accommodation, in hostels, hospitals, homes and schools. There is little published material, however, concerning this latter group and most psychological research has been aimed at studying the mentally handicapped to discover why requests for residential care are made, what effects institutions have and how residential care can best be provided.

Reasons for institutionalization

Several studies are available which indicate that there are identifiable factors which distinguish between those handicapped people for whom a request for residential care is made and those for whom it is not.

Intelligence level. Within the range of handicaps, parents' acceptance of normality of intelligence in their child produces attitudes against seeking residential care and there is some evidence that this is true of public attitudes too. Similarly, within the range of mental handicap, the lower the intelligence level, the more likely is a request for the person to be admitted to an institution of some kind. When those who live in hospitals are studied it is usually found that residents who have IQs below twenty are the most likely to have been admitted soon after they were diagnosed. Long-term admission, as opposed to a temporary admission which is requested for a short and usually predetermined time, is requested at a later stage as the intellectual level relatively increases.

Behaviour problems. Problems created by the behaviour of the handicapped person both inside and outside the home make a request for admission more likely. Outside the home, delinquent behaviour such as sexual offences, running away, fighting or stealing tend to lead to referral for admission and in this case the referral is often initiated by social agencies, such as social workers or probation officers, rather than by the parents, particularly if a court appearance is involved. Within the home it has been found to be active behaviour, such as aggressive behaviour towards parents, brothers and sisters or destructive activity involving damage to property, furnishings or objects around the house which is more likely to lead to a request for admission than passive, dependent behaviour.

Family background. Several family factors have been identified as related to admission requests. Broken homes where one parent has left, illegitimacy, inadequacy in the parents which makes them less able to run a home and control and care for their children, all tend to lead to conditions which make it more difficult to keep the handicapped person at home.

Another family factor has been described as the child's failure to meet parental expectations. Whether this condition applies will depend on how ambitious the parents are for their child, whether they have grown to have realistic or unrealistic expectations of his eventual level or whether they can accept his limitations. Failure to develop self-care skills is involved here and admission is more likely to be requested if the person is less able to look after himself as well as he is expected to by developing adequate feeding ability and eating habits, by being able to dress without supervision, by being able to keep himself reasonably clean and tidy, and by not being incontinent. Other ways in which parental expectations may not be met are if the child does not get on with his parents but is more disobedient, quarrelsome or defiant than they can accept or if the educational level he attains is below their expectations and he fails to learn to read or count or otherwise to progress academically.

Larger families have also been found more frequent in those cases where admission is requested and perhaps related to this is a further reason for wanting admission for a handicapped person, the needs of others in the family. When seeking admission, parents sometimes say that they feel they are spending much more time on a handicapped child than on their non-handicapped children and the latter are deprived of outings and attention they would otherwise receive. For the adult handicapped, when admission is sought because of the needs of the rest of the family, this tends to be because they need more care than the family is able to give, or more supervision than is possible, and the health and vigour of those looking after them becomes relevant.

It has been suggested that middle-class families are more likely to seek residential care but evidence does not seem very clear on this point and it appears likely that other factors are more important.

Provision of services. The more services that are available to and used by the handicapped person and his family, the less likely is a request for admission. Provisions like full diagnostic services and the availability of someone who can be asked for advice, speech therapy availability, school or workshop or some other facility where the handicapped person can go during the day, and recreation facilities like evening social clubs, all make it easier to keep the handicapped person at home Additionally, knowledge of residential accommodation and opinion as to its quality affects a parent's attitude to requesting it.

Other possible factors. There is disagreement as to the relevance of a few additional factors, in that they have been found relevant in some studies but not in others. Uncontrolled epilepsy is one such factor which has sometimes been thought to increase likelihood of admission. Others include the presence of physical anomalies where the handicapped person looks odd and is readily noticeable as handicapped, and family attitudes to retardation in general.

Defects in institution populations

Many studies have been concerned with the effects of being reared in an institution or spending later childhood there and a few have considered the advantages and disadvantages of hospital, hostel or community living for the adult handicapped person.

The main problem in evaluating the effects of living in an institution is that when comparing two groups, those living in an institution and those living at home, it is not always possible to say that at the point of time when the former group was institutionalized there was no relevant difference between them and those living at home. From the factors listed above it appears that there are many possible areas of difference between handicapped people who stay at home and those who leave, and it seems likely that those who go to residential accommodation were probably less acceptable to their parents in that they were developing more slowly, were less responsive, were more difficult to live with or perhaps their parents' attitudes towards them were different from the start. Some researchers have attempted to avoid this problem by studying people who have lived in residential care since they were babies and so were more likely to have been removed from their families by factors other than those appertaining to the characteristics of the child; even in this situation, however, the obviousness of their handicap may have differentiated them. Otherwise, attempts to avoid the problem that the groups may be pre-selected have consisted of carefully matching as many characteristics as possible between the group to be studied in the institution and the group at home.

Almost all studies have shown that a group living in a hospital is less well-developed and has more deficits than a comparable group living at home, when the groups are matched on factors like age, mental age and IQ. A few studies have investigated differences within institution groups and have found factors which relate to these differences which suggest the institutionalization is not the only factor which creates difficulties, but that life-experiences before admission are also relevant to later development.

There is evidence, however, that being in an institution is not always related to a lower level of functioning. Increases in IQs of the mildly mentally handicapped have been found when the residential environment is reasonably stimulating and when the person's home background is poor, and these increases are greatest for those whose backgrounds were most deprived. So for any particular person, whether the residential placement will have a detrimental or a beneficial effect is likely to depend on the conditions they have come from and the environment they are going to. There is evidence that there are differences between institutions in the degree to which they provide conditions conducive to the maximum development of their residents.

We shall now consider some of the areas where those living in hospitals have been found to be less well developed than those living at home.

Verbal skills

There is fairly general agreement that verbal development is more retarded in those in hospital than those living at home, particularly in children. The more developmentally advanced verbal skills tend to show a greater degree of retardation than those which appear earlier in the development of language. Smaller differences between the 'institution' and 'home' groups have been found in verbal comprehension and the use of single words, usually nouns, whereas sentence complexity and diversity, definition of words and range of speech sounds have shown wider differences between 'institution' and 'home' groups.

For example, one study (Lyle 1959) of two groups of severely retarded children, one living in a hospital and one living at home, found that there were no differences on non-verbal intelligence testing but highly significant differences on verbal subtests in favour of the group living at home and attending school daily. When the groups were divided into those children with Down's Syndrome and those with other diagnoses (because children with Down's Syndrome have on average less well-developed speech) it was found that Down's Syndrome children living at home were on average twelve months in advance of those living in the hospital on verbal tests, and those with other diagnoses living at home were on average six months in advance of those in hospital. The Down's Syndrome children in the hospital seemed most retarded in speech, as there was an average difference between them and the children with other diagnoses of nine months of verbal mental age whereas within the total group living at home there was no difference between those with Down's Syndrome and those with other diagnoses, and it was suggested that children with Down's Syndrome do less well in verbal areas in hospital.

It has rarely been possible to discover if the groups studied were of similar developmental level and comparable for the frequency of behaviour problems at the time one group went

126

into hospital, though it has been found that a child who is using speech when he goes into hospital tends to have better verbal scores later. However, if hospital living does retard speech development, possible causes are that children at home probably receive more active coaching in speech and more persuasion to use words or that they are able to benefit from being with brothers, sisters and friends who are of similar age but whose language development is greater.

Social behaviour

There are indications that any child, whether handicapped or non-handicapped, living in an uninteresting and unstimulating environment will show more immature behaviour and more behaviour concerned with himself and his own body rather than with other children and adults. In the context of social behaviour, institutions and the living conditions in them will be expected to vary and have different effects on behaviour according to how stimulating they are. The extreme apathy that was seen in institutionalized children a few decades ago when hospitals and children's homes were less equipped to meet children's needs is rarely seen now. However, observations suggest that handicapped children in hospitals tend to produce more diffuse movements and self-oriented behaviours, that is, they will engage in more activities which they can complete alone without the involvement of another person or an object, like rocking the body backwards and forwards, watching one's own hands or biting them, or running around with no obvious purpose. It has been suggested that if these behaviours become habitual, they may discourage development of more mature behaviour later and make it less likely that social relationships will be formed.

Various surveys have found that children in hospitals have fewer toys, are more likely to be restrained, have fewer experiences of social contact with adults and that the social contacts they do have are more varied than the child at home will experience. This means the child has fewer opportunities to get to know any one adult well. These factors interact with each other as social contact is known to stimulate exploration of objects, use of them and interest in them, and it has frequently been observed that a handicapped child needs an adult or older child to teach him to play by pointing out features of a toy, suggesting to him how he can play with it and showing approval when he manipulates it successfully.

Manipulative behaviour

Children in hospital have been found to be less able to handle and use small toys and less able to play constsuctively, through activities like building or completing puzzles. It seems likely that both of these are related to factors mentioned in the previous paragraph in that the availability of toys is likely to be less and they have fewer opportunities for learning to play with an adult. Providing an adequate supply of toys in a hospital ward is difficult and comparative lack of toys is not necessarily due to unwillingness to provide them. Amongst a group of handicapped children there are typically different levels of development and varying degrees of destructiveness. Supplies of toys tend to diminish with great rapidity when being used by a group and many toys which are suitable for the mentally handicapped child's developmental level are designed for smaller, less strong children to handle, though some toys specially designed for the mentally handicapped are now available.

Personality and emotional disturbance

A few studies have indicated differences in these areas. Children in hospitals have been found to be less assertive, less demanding and more passive. A greater number of those in hospitals have been considered emotionally disturbed. This latter finding is almost certainly related to the patients' state on admission as those who were disturbed had been admitted largely because of the disturbance. Within hospital populations it has been found that differences between those who are considered well-adjusted and those considered maladjusted relate to the age when the person left his parents and the degree to which contact has been maintained in that the better adjusted tend to have been admitted later and to have maintained contact with a parent.

Physical and motor development

Where physical measurements have been compared, children living at home have been found to be taller, heavier, to have greater leg length and calf circumference, and to have walked earlier. Conclusions on whether motor development is slower in those in hospital have varied, some studies showing there are no differences, others showing deficits in those in hospital. What is known is that when skills like walking are investigated, the quality of care in the institution is relevant. Children in institutions where they are cuddled and stimulated are likely to walk much earlier than those who have less stimulation.

Changes in institutions

Various changes have been instituted in residential settings to demonstrate possible ways of avoiding or ameliorating adverse effects of some features of institutions.

'Family' living

One way of providing extra stimulation and contact with adults for young children has been to house residents of different ages together, rather than to locate them in separate adult and children's wards. The aim is to achieve reciprocal benefits, for the children to receive attention and stimulation from the adult residents and for the adults to have the experience of caring for children. The system has been found to have advantages for very young children, in terms of developmental level, though little is known of the effects on adults.

Provision of 'Mothering'

One study showed that when a group of severely retarded boys were given intensive mothering, by being petted, cuddled and talked to, the boys increased in purposeful behaviour and showed less thumb-sucking and fewer badly co-ordinated movements. Another study demonstrated that by providing a consistent mother-figure, the social responsiveness of retarded children could be improved.

The Brooklands experiment

This project (Tizard 1964) demonstrated that the principles of care and education used in residential nurseries for normal children could be applied to the care of severely mentally handicapped children and that they would benefit. Sixteen children with mental ages between eighteen months and five years who were living in a hospital for the mentally handicapped were moved to a large house to live. The hospital they lived in was old and over-crowded and daily living was affected by the problems and needs of the hospital, so that they tended to be fed, dressed and toileted all at the same time in a large group and to have inadequate opportunity for play. At Brooklands they lived in smaller groups with more continuous care from the same member of staff looking after them. A teacher who used nursery school methods was provided and toys were chosen to be appropriate to the children's needs. In general, the facilities and atmosphere were designed to be much more like a home than a hospital and to be more child-centred. Results of the project which ran for two years indicated that the children had benefited from the improved living conditions. Measures of their verbal mental age showed that it had increased by an average of ten months whilst they had been at Brooklands whereas the average increase in a control group still at the hospital was four months.

The E6 experiment

Following the Brooklands project, Stephen and Robertson (1972) applied the same principles to a ward in a children's hospital. The mental age range of the twenty children who lived on ward E6 was lower than that of the children who went to Brooklands, being from six months to three and a half years. At the beginning of the experiment the children were between two and eleven years old. As with the Brooklands group, the children were divided into two smaller groups for daily living, each group having a cross-section of age, sex and degree of handicap and nurses were attached mainly to one group. Weekly meetings to report each child's progress were held with ward staff and consistency of handling was improved by having a progress chart and a list of words used with each child prominently displayed. 'Aunties', who were volunteer visitors, were found for children who had no relatives who visited and quarterly meetings were held for parents and 'aunties'. Other features of the ward were provision of a junk box, containing items which a normal child would find lying around in a home but which need to be consciously provided in a ward, early evening play sessions with girls from a local grammar school, individual clothing for each child and an attempt to provide individual toys, frequent outings and an adventure playground. Those with mental ages over two years went to school and were taught by a nursery school teacher, the others had a play programme on the ward, designed to be appropriate to their mental level. When the experiment had continued for three years results showed that the children had benefited – when they were compared with similar children on other wards – in mental development and ability to look after themselves, though progress had been made mostly by those whose mental ages were above two years.

Varieties of residential provision

Current attitudes are in favour of reducing the size of large hospitals for the handicapped and providing more accommodation for handicapped people who cannot live at home in hostels within the community. Large hospitals are often surrounded by extensive grounds and geographically isolated from the nearest town and it is felt that handicapped people can become more integrated into society if they live nearer to everyone else. Hostels can provide a background for living much more like that of a normal home than is possible in a traditional hospital which has large living and dormitory areas joined by corridors.

Although community hostels are intended to help reduce the size of hospitals by allowing transfer of those who are in hospital but are capable of living in a hostel, there is some evidence that hostels are at present being used more for direct admissions from the community. These admissions are mainly because of death, hospitalization, illness or incapacity of the mother or whoever looks after the handicapped person and to a lesser extent are due to behaviour problems of the person being admitted. Hence, hostels are probably admitting people who would have gone to a hospital if no hostel were available, and so far are thus indirectly reducing the size of hospitals, but at present there seem to be too few hostels to make rapid reductions in hospital size.

Independence in hostels

Hostels vary in their criteria for admission from those which take any child from a given area regardless of developmental level or behaviour to those which require residents to work in open employment. However, many are intended to provide opportunity for a more independent way of living than is usual in hospitals. There are indications, however, that in some cases the hostel residents are more overprotected and assisted than they need to be, and that not all hostels are fulfilling a function of promoting independence. One comparison of hospital and hostel residents showed that when assessed and reassessed twelve months later, although the hostel residents had far greater attainments in self-care on both occasions, the hospital residents showed significant increases during the year whereas the hostel residents did not. This was felt to be partly due to the higher level of attainment of the hostel residents which allowed less scope for improvements, but more attributable to a tendency for some hostel staff to do things for the residents that they could have learned to do for themselves.

When independence is encouraged and achieved in hostels a problem may arise when a resident becomes independent to a degree where he no longer needs hostel care. He may easily become so comfortable in the hostel that he is reluctant to move on to more independent living which both halts his own progress and prevents another person using the hostel place. Alternatively he may be reluctant to leave as he knows no one in the community and would feel lonely alone in lodgings away from the hostel group. One solution to the problem of where residents should go from hostels is the provision of group homes. These are ordinary houses rented or purchased by local authorities, voluntary societies or hospitals where a small group, usually five or six, lives. To date, there are only a few of these provided for the mentally handicapped, but although some residents have not been successfully placed in them, the majority are running well. Most of the mentally handicapped who live in group homes are mildly mentally handicapped and total independence in self-care is expected. However, a considerable amount of support tends to be given, in comparison with the amount given to group homes for the mentally ill. Most have frequent visits from social workers, maintain hospital contacts and usually have domestic help provided.

Family contacts
Being in a hostel often enables a handicapped person to have more contact with his family, and placing a person in a hostel within ten miles of his family, provided that the family is interested in him, has been shown to increase contacts. It has been found that only a minority of hostel residents have friends outside the hostel but an even smaller minority of hospital residents do.

Residents' attitudes to hostels
Campbell (1968) interviewed 252 mentally handicapped and sixty-four mentally ill hostel residents. 57 per cent had moved to the hostel from a hospital and 43 per cent from

the community, either from home or other residential accommodation. She found that 53 per cent preferred to live in the hostel and 19 per cent preferred their previous residence (8 per cent gave no clear preference). There were differences between those who had previously lived in hospital and those who came from home. Of the former group, 88 per cent preferred the hostel to hospital and only 7 per cent preferred their previous residence. Those who came from home were more evenly divided; 40 per cent preferred the hostel and 48 per cent preferred their previous residence. Those who preferred hostel to hospital most commonly said that this was because they were freer in the hostel and could go out when they liked, some said that the hostel was nearer their family and others preferred the material comforts or the staff of the hostel. Of the small number who preferred the hospital, six gave no reason, three said it was because their friends were there, two had had quarrels with other hostel residents and one, in a mixed hostel, found it too noisy being with girls.

Residents were also asked if they preferred having a single bedroom or sharing a room. More of those who came from home preferred single rooms than those from hospital, and reasons for preferring a single room were that it was more private, quieter and could be arranged as the resident wanted it. Those who preferred sharing a bedroom did so mainly because they liked company.

Aiming at normality

Underlying current trends of residential care, whether in hospital or hostel, are towards providing the handicapped person with as normal a life as possible.

The same aim underlies the entire field of the psychology of handicap: to see how far we can aim at normality for the handicapped person and how we can give him what most other people have.

We aim to discover what skills and attainments he needs, how he can best be taught them and how we can help him to adapt as normally as possible to his surroundings. We aim to discover how his surroundings, the facilities provided, the family he lives in and the attitudes surrounding him affect him and how they can be changed to increase his opportunities of normality.

Aiming at normality does not mean that the limitations

imposed by the handicap should be ignored but that they should be accepted as a starting point with normality, even if we feel it can never be achieved, as a principle to indicate direction.

Appendix:
A description of
handicaps

The following notes are brief descriptions of the handicaps referred to in the volume and are intended to enable the reader to understand the type, variety and extent of the handicaps involved in each condition, rather than to be full etiological and medical definitions.

Autism, also referred to as 'infantile psychosis', 'early infantile autism', 'childhood schizophrenia' and 'childhood psychosis', is a condition characterized by several symptoms, of which the autistic child has some but not necessarily all. These symptoms include self-sufficient behaviour and poor emotional relationships with others, lack of or impaired speech, a tendency to ritualistic behaviour or mannerisms – like an abnormal attachment to one object or a tendency to arrange objects in straight lines or other fixed patterns, inappropriate response to sensory stimuli, insistence on a fixed routine and resistance to change, and 'islands' of intelligent functioning in an otherwise retarded background. The cause is currently unknown. There is sometimes disagreement on diagnosis of an individual case. The term is often applied only if symptoms occur before two years of age.

Cerebral palsy is a general term applied to a group of conditions resulting from damage to the developing brain which may have occurred before, during or after birth. The main feature is a loss of control over voluntary body movements. The condition is of varying severity, from mild and hardly noticeable, perhaps affecting one limb only, to severe and almost totally incapacitating. The term 'spasticity' is sometimes used as synonymous with 'cerebral palsy' but, used more strictly, refers to the most common of these conditions (over half) where the voluntary muscles overcontract and the limbs, eyes and tongue are stiff and difficult to control. The second commonest form, athetosis (about a quarter), is characterized by constant writhing movements.

Epilepsy refers to episodes of disturbance in the functioning of the brain which may involve temporary loss of consciousness, convulsions or changes in sensation, movement, involuntary functions, mental or emotional state. In a majority of cases, no specific cause is found; in some, epilepsy is produced by an identifiable condition affecting the brain, like injury, disease, inflammation, or tumour. Much epilepsy can be well-controlled by modern drugs.

Grand mal epilepsy usually involves loss of consciousness, falling to the ground, and jerking or twitching of the body. Petit mal epilepsy is less noticeable and usually involves a brief loss of consciousness when the person may stop what he is doing, drop what he is holding or stop speaking. Other types of epilepsy involve trance-like behaviour, episodes of confusion or one-sided convulsions.

Hearing impairment includes deafness and partial hearing. Again the degree varies; the impairment may be almost complete, the person may be able to hear some levels of sound but not others or be generally a little hard of hearing.

Limb deficiency involves absence or underdevelopment of one or more limbs, where the limbs have never developed. The most well-known group of congenitally limb deficient children are those whose condition is due to use of the drug thalidomide as a sedative or antidote to nausea during the mother's pregnancy before the effects of the drug on unborn children were known; in the case of these children, there were many abnormalities including hands attached to shoulders and feet attached to hips.

Mental handicap involves retarded mental development in varying degrees. The mildly mentally handicapped are mostly not in need of special help, only a minority have problems and many are not readily identifiable as handicapped. The severely mentally handicapped rarely attain complete independence and usually need a degree of assistance and protected living. In many cases, a definite cause cannot be established. The largest identifiable group of the severely mentally handicapped, where definite diagnosis can be made, is that of Down's Syndrome (mongolism) which is due to a genetic defect from the time of conception.

Mental illness is a condition which usually implies that behaviour and capacity for living a normal life have previously been unimpaired in contrast to mental handicap where the condition is usually present from birth. Mental illness tends to involve primarily disturbances in emotional state and abnormalities in behaviour whereas the main features of mental handicap are limited intellectual development and retarded behaviour. A mental illness may be of short duration, may recur periodically or have lasting effects, but mental handicap is a long-term and generally permanent condition.

Muscular dystrophy includes several conditions. The type referred to in this volume, and the one which mostly affects children, is known as Duchenne type, or progressive muscular dystrophy. It mostly affects males and is characterized by a progressive weakening and wasting of the muscles, the abnormality arising in the muscle and not in the nervous system. Symptoms begin in the first ten years and life expectancy is much reduced, death usually occurring in the twenties. The cause is genetic and for a mother who has this gene, half of her sons are at risk for having muscular dystrophy and half of her daughters are likely to carry the gene.

Spina bifida is a defect in the spinal cord where the vertebral canal and usually the spinal cord are incompletely closed. The severity of the condition varies with the position and extent of the defect, and may be virtually unnoticeable or severely handicapping. When the nerves lying in the spinal cord are exposed, hydrocephalus, an increase in the volume of cerebrospinal fluid within the skull, may occur. Problems associated with spina bifida again depend on the position of the lesion and are particularly incontinence and inability to walk due to paralysis of the legs.

Visual impairment includes blindness and partial sight and varies in severity from total inability to see to a degree of difficulty which affects everyday life.

References
and Name Index

The numbers in italics after each entry refer
to page numbers within this book.

Bagley, C. (1971) *The Social Psychology of the Child with Epilepsy* (London, Routledge and Kegan Paul). *84, 89, 114*

Bolton, B. (1972) 'Psychometric Validation of a Clinically Derived Typology of Deaf Rehabilitation Clients', *Journal of Clinical Psychology, 28* (1): 22–5. *82*

Burchard, J. D. and Barrera, F. (1972) 'An Analysis of Time-out and Response Cost in a Programmed Environment', *Journal of Applied Behaviour Analysis, 5* (3): 271–82. *92*

Campbell, A. C. (1968) 'Attitudes of Mentally Disordered Adults to Community Care', *British Journal of Preventative and Social Medicine, 22*: 94–9. *132*

Cashdan, A. (1968) 'Mothers Bringing up Physically Handicapped Children', in Loring, J. and Mason, A. (eds) *The Subnormal Child* (London, The Spastics Society). *59*

Clarke, A. M. and Clarke, A. D. B. (1974) *Mental Deficiency: The Changing Outlook* (London, Methuen). *34*

Cohen, H. J., Molnar, G. E. and Taft, L. T. (1968) 'The Genetic Relationship of Progressive Muscular Dystrophy (Duchenne Type) and Mental Retardation', *Developmental Medicine and Child Neurology, 10*: 754–765. *78*

Colin, D. and Vurpillot E. (1971–72) 'Influence of Deafness on Visual Perceptual Organization of Children of Pre-school Age', *Bulletin de Psychologie, 25* (14–17): 882–887. *75*

Colwell, C. N., Richards, E., McCarver, R. B. and Ellis, N. R. (1973) 'Evaluation of Self-Help Habit Training of the Profoundly Retarded', *Mental Retardation*, pp. 14–18. *118*

Connolly, K. (1968) 'Operant Methods for Training Subnormal and Handicapped Children', in Loring, J. and Mason, A. (eds, *The Subnormal Child* (London, The Spastics Society). *120*

Cowen, E. L. and Bobrove, P. H. (1966) 'Marginality of Disability and Adjustment', *Perceptual and Motor Skills*, *23*: 869–70. *25*

Cromwell, R. (1963) 'A Social Learning Approach to Mental Retardation', in Ellis, N. R., *Handbook of Mental Deficiency* (New York, McGraw-Hill). *82*

Cumming, E. and Cumming, J. (1957) *Closed Ranks: An Experiment in Mental Health* (Cambridge, Mass., Harvard University Press). *41*

Dalton, A. J., Rubino, C. A. and Hislop, M. W. (1973) 'Some Effects of Token Awards on School Achievement of Children with Down's Syndrome', *Journal of Applied Behaviour Analysis*, *6* (2): 251–9. *115*

Dershowitz, N. K. (1973) 'On Tactual Perception of Physiognomic Properties', *Perceptual and Motor Skills*, *36*: 343–55. *73*

Dunsdon, M. I. (1952) *The Educability of Cerebral Palsied Children*. (London: Newnes). *75*

Goffman, E. (1968) *Stigma* (New Jersey, Prentice Hall 1963 and Harmondsworth, Penguin 1968). *38*

Gorton, C. E. (1972) 'The Effects of Various Classroom Environments on Performance of a Mental Task by Mentally Retarded and Normal Children', *Education and Training of the Mentally Retarded*, *7* (1): 32–38. *74*

Guralnick, M. J. and Kravik, M. A. (1973) 'Reinforcement Procedures and Social Behaviour in a Group Context with Severely Retarded Children', *Psychological Reports*, *32*: 295–301. *117*

Halliday, M. J., Rawlings, H. E. M. and Whipp, M. A. (1965) 'The Spina Bifida/Hydrocephalic Child in the Community', *The Practitioner*, *195*: 346–50. *52*

Heber, R., Garber H., Harrington, S., and Falender, C. (1972) *Rehabilitation of Families at Risk for Mental Retardation: Progress Report* (Rehabilitation Research and Training Centre in Mental Retardation, University of Wisconsin). *112*

Hewett, S. (1970) *The Family and the Handicapped Child* (London, George Allen & Unwin). *11, 48, 55–8. 60, 61, 62, 63, 83*

Jones, J. (1965) 'Employment of Epileptics', *Lancet*, *II*: 486–9. *26*

Lotter, V. (1966) 'Epidemiology of Autistic Conditions in Young Children I: Prevalence,' *Social Psychiatry*, *1*: 124–137. *71*

Lyle, J. G. (1959) 'The Effect of an Institution Environment upon the Verbal Development of Imbecile Children', *Journal of Mental Deficiency Research*, *3* (2): 122–8. *126*

Meyerson L., Kerr, N. and Michael J. L. (1967), 'Behaviour Modification in Rehabilitation' in Bijou, S. W. and Baer, D. M. (eds) *Child Development; Readings in Experimental Analysis* (New York, Appleton-Century-Crofts). *121*

O'Connor, N. and Yonge, K. A. (1955) 'Methods of Evaluating the Group Psychotherapy of Unstable Defective Delinquents', *Genet. Psychol. 87*: 89–101. *90*

Ringness, T. A. (1961) 'Self-Concept of Children of Low, Average and High Intelligence', *American Journal of Mental Deficiency, 65*: 453–61. *24*

Roskies, E. (1972) *Abnormality and Normality: The Mothering of Thalidomide Children* (Ithaca and London, Cornell University Press). *47, 52*

Rutter, M., Greenfield, D. and Lockyer, L. (1967) 'A Five to Fifteen Year Follow-up Study of Infantile Psychosis', *British Journal of Psychiatry, 113*: 1169–82. *71*

Rutter, M., Tizard, J. and Whitmore, K. (1970) *Education, Health and Behaviour* (London, Longman). *11, 54, 56, 57, 61, 68, 70, 76*

Snyder, R. and Sechrist, L. (1959) 'Experimental Study of Directive Group Therapy with Defective Delinquents', *Amer. J. Ment. Defic. 64*: 117–123. *91*

Stephen, E. and Robertson, J. (1972) 'Growing Up in Hospital: A Study of the Care of Severely Mentally Handicapped Children in a Comprehensive Children's Hospital', *Mental Retardation: Occasional Papers*, No. 2/4 (London, Butterworths). *19, 130*

Tierney, A. J. (1973) 'Toilet Training', *Nursing Times*, Dec. 20/27, pp. 1740–4. *119*

Tizard, J. (1964) *Community Services for the Mentally Handicapped* (Oxford University Press). *129*

Wilcox, R. and Smith, J. L. (1973) 'Some Psychological–Social Correlates of Mental Retardation', *Perceptual and Motor Skills, 36*: 999–1006. *82*

Wooster, A. D. (1970) 'Formation of Stable and Discrete Concepts of Personality by Normal and Mentally Retarded Boys', *Journal of Mental Subnormality, 16* (30): 24–8. *23*

Subject Index

142